T0222285

Introducing ReScript

Functional Programming for Web Applications

Danny Yang

Apress®

Introducing ReScript: Functional Programming for Web Applications

Danny Yang
Mountain View, CA, USA

ISBN-13 (pbk): 978-1-4842-8887-0   ISBN-13 (electronic): 978-1-4842-8888-7
https://doi.org/10.1007/978-1-4842-8888-7

Managing Director, Apress Media LLC: Welmoed Spahr
Acquisitions Editor: Steve Anglin
Development Editor: James Markham
Coordinating Editor: Jill Balzano

Cover designed by eStudioCalamar

Cover image by Steve Johnson on Unsplash (www.unsplash.com)

Distributed to the book trade worldwide by Apress Media, LLC, 1 New York Plaza, New York, NY 10004, U.S.A. Phone 1-800-SPRINGER, fax (201) 348-4505, e-mail orders-ny@springer-sbm.com, or visit www.springeronline.com. Apress Media, LLC is a California LLC and the sole member (owner) is Springer Science + Business Media Finance Inc (SSBM Finance Inc). SSBM Finance Inc is a **Delaware** corporation.

For information on translations, please e-mail booktranslations@springernature.com; for reprint, paperback, or audio rights, please e-mail bookpermissions@springernature.com.

Apress titles may be purchased in bulk for academic, corporate, or promotional use. eBook versions and licenses are also available for most titles. For more information, reference our Print and eBook Bulk Sales web page at http://www.apress.com/bulk-sales.

Any source code or other supplementary material referenced by the author in this book is available to readers on GitHub (https://github.com/Apress). For more detailed information, please visit http://www.apress.com/source-code.

Printed on acid-free paper

Table of Contents

About the Author

Danny Yang is a professional software engineer at Meta working on infrastructure for WhatsApp. He has previously worked on Facebook Messenger, including the web interface which was written in ReScript. His technical interests include functional programming, compilers, and data visualization, which he writes about on his blog at `www.yangdanny97` `.github.io`.

About the Technical Reviewer

German Gonzalez-Morris is a software architect/engineer working with C/C++, Java, and different application containers, in particular with WebLogic Server. He has developed various applications using JEE, Spring, and Python. His areas of expertise also include OOP, Java/JEE, Python, design patterns, algorithms, Spring Core/MVC/security, and microservices. German has worked with performance messaging, RESTful API, and transactional systems. For more information about him, visit www.linkedin.com/in/german-gonzalez-morris.

Introduction

Why Learn ReScript?

JavaScript is vital to the modern web ecosystem. It's used in the front end to implement websites and other user interfaces, and used in the back end to implement servers for websites and APIs.

Part of JavaScript's ubiquity is due to its ease of use. JavaScript is dynamic and flexible, making it easy for people to pick up. However, this strength becomes a weakness when working on large web applications with multiple developers – the only way to know that JavaScript code works correctly is to actually run it, and it's relatively easy to make mistakes when programming in JavaScript.

What if there was a way to detect bugs in JavaScript before running the code, or prevent many classes of bugs altogether? What if there was a language that was concise and elegant that made it easy for programmers to write complex web applications and hard for programmers to make mistakes?

Enter ReScript.

ReScript is a language designed for writing web applications. It brings a lot to the table: static typechecking, a strong type system, and powerful language features that will change the way you program.

Here's a glimpse of some of the features that make ReScript a great language:

Static typechecking – Catch bugs in your code without having to run it: undefined values, missing cases, incorrect types, and more.

Sound type system – ReScript programs that pass typechecking cannot have runtime type errors.

Type inference – ReScript automatically infers types based on how variables are used, allowing you to enjoy the benefits of type safety without having to annotate every variable and function.

Immutability – Peace of mind while you program with variables and data structures that cannot be unexpectedly modified under your nose.

Algebraic data types and pattern matching – Cleanly define and elegantly manipulate complex data.

First-class bindings for React – Write React elements and JSX directly inside ReScript files.

There are a number of other languages and tools that offer static typechecking for web applications, but ReScript has several key advantages over its competitors. As an example, let's look at the benefits ReScript has compared with another popular JavaScript alternative, TypeScript:

ReScript is safer – Unlike ReScript's battle-tested and sound type system, TypeScript's type system is unsound, so it is still possible to have runtime type errors in a valid TypeScript program.

ReScript is faster – ReScript's compiler is much faster than TypeScript's compiler, allowing for a smoother development experience when working in large code bases.

ReScript is more concise – ReScript's excellent type inference means that programmers do not have to write as many type annotations in ReScript programs compared to TypeScript programs.

Although ReScript is a relative newcomer to the web ecosystem, it's actually based on technology that has been battle-tested for years before ReScript even existed. ReScript itself has proven successful as well. Most notably, Facebook used it to build the web interface for Messenger – a product used by hundreds of millions of people – with a code base containing thousands of files.

History of ReScript

The lineage of ReScript can ultimately be traced back to the ML family of languages originating from the 1960s. In particular, ReScript is directly based on OCaml, a general-purpose programming language that was developed in the 1980s and used today for systems programming in academia and industry.

In 2015, Jordan Walke, the creator of the React web framework, developed a toolchain and alternative syntax for OCaml called Reason.

Reason was designed to bridge the gap between the web and OCaml ecosystems – it could be compiled into both native machine code and JavaScript, allowing web developers to take advantage of OCaml's features. Static typechecking and OCaml's sound type system eliminated many common bugs in JavaScript code, and OCaml's immutability and functional style was a great fit for React.

Reason was compiled to JavaScript using a compiler called BuckleScript, which was developed at Bloomberg around the same time Reason was being created at Facebook.

Around 2020, the BuckleScript project created a new language based on Reason that could only be compiled to JavaScript using the BuckleScript compiler, and so ReScript was born.

ReScript has the following key differences from its predecessors:

> **ReScript has different syntax and features**. While it looks and feels more like JavaScript, ReScript is still based on the battle-tested compiler and type system as Reason and OCaml, so it has the same type safety benefits as its predecessors.

> **ReScript can only be compiled to JavaScript**. By dropping support for native compilation, ReScript has a simpler toolchain and standard library, along with a feature set better suited for web development. This makes ReScript easier for newcomers to learn and allows for smoother integration with other web technologies.

ReScript and the Web Ecosystem

Like some other statically typed languages in the web ecosystem, ReScript code is transpiled to JavaScript. This means that ReScript code doesn't directly run in the browser or on the server. Instead, the ReScript compiler checks that the code is valid and generates JavaScript files, which can then be imported and used like any handwritten JavaScript file.

Being able to run in any environment that supports JavaScript allows ReScript to be used for full-stack web development, from client-side code that runs in the browser to server-side code that runs in Node.js.

Since ReScript code is exactly the same as JavaScript code when it runs, ReScript programs can easily import and use JavaScript libraries, while JavaScript programs can call ReScript functions as easily as they can call other JavaScript functions.

Why Learn Functional Programming?

Functional programming is a paradigm of programming that focuses on the application and composition of functions.

In functional languages, functions are first class and can be used like any other value (bound to variables, passed as arguments, or returned from other functions). Complex programs are written by composing multiple smaller functions that apply transformations to data. This can be contrasted with the imperative and object-oriented style of many popular languages, where programs look more like a series of commands that read and update memory. It's important to know that most languages are not purely in one category or the other; many languages fall somewhere in the middle of this spectrum, and features from functional languages are slowly being adopted by other languages. For example, ReScript is more functional but it also has imperative features like loops, while JavaScript is more imperative but it also has first-class functions.

Programming in a functional style has many benefits – programs are cleaner and more concise, and logic is more declarative making it easier to trace the flow of data through a program. The ability to compose functions together and write functions that accept other functions as arguments (higher-order functions) makes functional languages very flexible, and the greater emphasis on immutability and purity makes it easier to understand, write, and test programs.

As a disclaimer, I'm not some functional programming purist here to convince you that functional programming is the best way to solve every problem. Instead, I view functional programming as a useful tool in a programmer's tool belt, albeit a tool that not enough people know about or know how to use.

Unlike many other functional programming books, the explanations in this book are designed to be accessible to those without a formal background in computer science. I do not expect readers to have experience with statically typed languages or functional programming concepts.

About This Book

This book is written for anyone who is interested in learning ReScript or wants to learn the basics of functional programming using ReScript.

The book is structured as an overview of ReScript's features, building up from the basics to eventually cover complex data types, pattern matching, modules, and finally writing a minimal web application using ReScript.

Along the way, you will learn functional programming concepts like higher-order functions, immutability, and purity, which will help you think about and write software differently, even when you are not using ReScript.

Here's what this book will cover:

Chapter 1 – Language basics: expressions, binding, and control flow

Chapter 2 – Functions: higher-order programming, recursion, and purity

Chapter 3 – Composite data types, pattern matching, and error handling

Chapter 4 – Records and objects

Chapter 5 – Lists and arrays: map, filter, and reduce

Chapter 6 – Collections: sets, maps, stacks, and queues

Chapter 7 – Modular programming: modules and functors

Chapter 8 – JavaScript integrations: bindings, dealing with JSON, and more

Installing ReScript

ReScript projects are set up just like modern JavaScript projects, except we have an extra development dependency on the rescript package.

Before we begin, make sure you have Node.js v10 or higher, and npm. To check the version of Node.js you have, run node -v in your terminal. If you don't have Node.js installed, you can find installation instructions at https://nodejs.org.

Once you've confirmed that you have the right version of Node.js installed, create a new directory for your project, and run npm install rescript@10 to install v10 of ReScript.

There will be a package.json file with the following contents inside the project's root directory. Add the following scripts to it:

```
{
  ...

  "scripts": {
      "build": "rescript",
      "start": "rescript build -w"
  }
}
```

The scripts we added in package.json are used to run the ReScript compiler to compile our ReScript to JavaScript.

> **npm run build** will compile all the ReScript files in the project.
>
> **npm run start** will start a process that watches the project and automatically recompiles whenever anything changes.

Next, create a bsconfig.json file inside the same directory, with the following contents:

```
{
  "name": "your-project-name",
  "sources": [
    {
      "dir": "src",
      "subdirs": true
    }
  ],
  "package-specs": [
    {
      "module": "commonjs",
      "in-source": true
    }
  ],
  "suffix": ".bs.js",
  "bs-dependencies": []
}
```

The dir field specifies which directory ReScript source files are located, in this case under the folder src. For every ReScript file Foo.res under src, the compiler will output a JavaScript file named Foo.bs.js in the same location as the original source.

Now we're ready to write some ReScript!

First ReScript Program

Source files in ReScript have the extension `.res`. We can write a simple Hello World program by creating a file at `src/HelloWorld.res` with the following contents:

```
Js.log("hello, world")
```

ReScript is a compiled language – this means that the ReScript files that we write are not being run directly by the browser or Node.js. The compiler checks to make sure our ReScript code is valid – syntax is correct, function calls and values are the right types, etc. – and then it compiles the ReScript files into JavaScript. The browser or Node.js will run the JavaScript the same way they would for JavaScript we wrote by hand.

Run the compiler using `npm run build`. You will see the compiled output in `src/HelloWorld.bs.js`, which will have the following contents:

```
console.log("hello, world");
```

You can run the JavaScript file using `node src/HelloWorld.bs.js` to print "hello, world" to the terminal.

Since ReScript compiles to JavaScript, it can be used for both client and server applications in a variety of environments – your browser, Node.js, etc. For the purposes of this book, we will be executing ReScript programs in Node.js.

As you read through the examples in the book, I encourage you to copy the examples into your code editor or the ReScript playground at `https://rescript-lang.org/try` so that you can compile and run the programs yourself. As you experiment with ReScript for yourself, make sure to inspect the compiled JavaScript output of your ReScript programs to get a deeper understanding of how ReScript works under the hood. You'll find that the generated JavaScript code is quite readable!

CHAPTER 1

ReScript Basics

In this chapter, we'll dive right into the basic concepts of ReScript: expressions, values, control flow, and binding. At the end of the chapter, we'll use those concepts in a simple command-line program.

Expressions, Values, and Side Effects

Expressions are the fundamental building block of ReScript programs. In this section, we will be going over basic expressions in ReScript and their **semantics** – their meaning. Just like we can learn the English language by studying the meaning of words and sentences, we can learn ReScript by studying the meaning of expressions.

In general, we will think about semantics like this: Evaluating an expression performs some computation and yields a single **result**. The result is a **value**, or something that cannot be evaluated any further – for example, the expression 2 + 3 evaluates to 5. Additionally, the evaluation might produce any number of **side effects**, or changes that can be observed outside of the function – for example, evaluating an expression can mutate an array, print something to the console, or throw an exception.

In other languages, computation can be modeled as both expressions and statements, where expressions yield a value when evaluated and statements do not. In ReScript, there is no such thing as statements, and every expression will yield a value if evaluated successfully.

© Danny Yang 2023
D. Yang, *Introducing ReScript*, https://doi.org/10.1007/978-1-4842-8888-7_1

Compile Time and Runtime

To differentiate between things that happen when the ReScript code is compiled and when the resulting JavaScript code is actually run, we'll introduce the terms **compile time** and **runtime**.

Again using 2 + 3 as an example:

> **At compile time**, the ReScript compiler checks that 2 and 3 are valid numbers and can be added together. Then, it outputs JavaScript code, which in this simple case is also 2 + 3.

> **At runtime**, the JavaScript code actually runs and 2 + 3 is evaluated to 5.

The code snippets in this book will sometimes be followed by the expected output of the snippet. Outputs at compile time will be labeled as "Compiler output," and outputs at runtime will be labeled as "Console output."

Types, Typechecking, and Type Inference

Just like how values in JavaScript have types like number, object, and boolean, expressions and values in ReScript also have types. In JavaScript, types are not very strict, and values may be interpreted as different types depending on the context they are being used in. In contrast, types in ReScript are more strict.

In a compile-time process called **static typechecking**, the compiler checks that the types of expressions and functions in our program are consistent with each other, allowing us to catch potential bugs without needing to run the program.

To help the typechecker, the programmer can write down what type each variable or function is supposed to be – this is called a **type annotation**. Unlike other languages with static typechecking, type annotations in ReScript are usually optional, thanks to a feature called **type inference** which automatically detects the type of expressions or functions based on how they are used.

Whether or not a programmer chooses to annotate types is a trade-off between clarity and conciseness – type annotations take time to write, but they can help make the code easier for other people to read.

In this book, you'll learn the names of types and how to write type annotations, but not every example will be fully annotated.

Primitive Types and Operators

Integer and Float

Unlike JavaScript which only has a single type for numbers (number), there are two types of numbers in ReScript: integers and floats (int and float).

Integers in ReScript are limited to 32 bits, while floats in ReScript are identical to JavaScript numbers.

They have different sets of arithmetic operators:

Int operators – +, -, *, /

Float operators – +., -., *., /., **

ReScript's type system is strict, so integer arithmetic operators can only be used on two integers, and float arithmetic operators can only be used on two floats.

Integers may be converted to floats using float() or Belt.Int.toFloat(); the opposite conversion can be done using int_of_float() or Belt.Int.fromFloat().

Additionally, there are a few operations that are done using functions instead of operators:

Js.Math.pow_int(x, y) is the equivalent of ** for integers

mod(x, y) remainder/modulo for integers

land(x, y) bitwise logical AND for integers

lor(x, y) bitwise logical OR for integers

lxor(x, y) bitwise logical XOR for integers

lnot(x) bitwise logical NOT for integers

lsl(x, y) left shift for integers

lsr(x, y) logical right shift for integers

asr(x, y) arithmetic right shift for integers

Here are some examples of int and float arithmetic operators and their equivalents in JavaScript:

ReScript	JavaScript
1+1	1+1
1.0 +. 1.0	1.0 + 1.0
1.0 +. float(1)	1.0 + 1
2.0 ** 3.0	Math.pow(2.0, 3.0)
float(2) ** float(3)	Math.pow(2, 3)

Other standard library functions for ints and floats are found in the Belt.Int, Belt.Float, Js.Int, Js.Float, and Js.Math modules. The latter contains many useful utilities like random numbers, rounding, trigonometry, and more.

Integers are convenient to use when representing small numbers in ReScript programs – they support more operations and their operators feel more natural. However, we should always use floats to represent very large whole numbers (such as unix timestamps) – using integer operations on those numbers will truncate them to 32 bits!

Boolean

The boolean values `true` and `false` in ReScript are exactly the same as booleans in JavaScript. Unlike in JavaScript, there is no such thing as interpreting non-boolean values like numbers or strings as "truthy" and "falsy" in ReScript – the only possible values for the `bool` type are `true` and `false`. Furthermore, only boolean values may be passed to conditionals and boolean operators, like `while`, `if`, `&&`, `||`, etc.

Here are some common boolean operators:

Logical AND, OR, NOT: `&&`, `||`, `!`

Comparison operators: `>`, `<`, `>=`, `<=`

Structural equality: `==`, `!=`

Referential equality: `===`, `!==`

Structural equality is a deep comparison of the values of nested objects – two objects are structurally equal if they have the same fields and the values of all the corresponding fields are structurally equal, and two arrays are structurally equal if they have the same number elements and the corresponding elements are structurally equal.

On the other hand, **referential equality** evaluates to true if both sides are actually the same object.

For example:

`{ "a": 1 } == { "a": 1 }` evaluates to `true`.

`{ "a": 1 } === { "a": 1 }` evaluates to `false`.

5

[1, 1] == [1, 1] evaluates to true.

[1, 1] === [1, 1] evaluates to false.

x == x evaluates to true.

x === x evaluates to true.

Note that equality operators can only be used on two values that are the same type; for example, the expression 1 == "2" is not allowed and will result in the following typechecker error:

```
This has type: string
Somewhere wanted: int
```

String

String literals in ReScript are written with double quotes and may span multiple lines. Strings can be concatenated using the ++ operator.

To convert other primitive values to strings, use the toString functions in the standard library – for example, Js.Int.toString, Js.Float. toString, etc. Here is an example of string concatenation and conversion:

```
"I am " ++ Js.Int.toString(5) ++ " years old"
```

Here is an example of slicing a string using the standard library:

```
// this expression evaluates to "34"
Js.String2.slice("12345", ~from=2, ~to_=4)
```

ReScript supports string interpolation, although with the restriction that interpolated expressions must all be strings. The string concatenation example implemented using interpolation would look like this:

```
`I am ${Js.Int.toString(5)} years old`
```

The standard library functions for strings are found in the `Js.String2` module – for the most part, these functions are exactly the same as the JavaScript function with the same name.

In JavaScript, we might trim and split a string like this:

```
let s = "  1,2,3,4,5  "
let s2 = s.trim().split(",")
```

In ReScript, we can do the same using functions in `Js.String2` (don't worry about the arrow syntax for now, that will be explained in the next chapter):

```
let s = "  1,2,3,4,5  "
let s2 = s->Js.String2.trim->Js.String2.split(",")
```

Unit

ReScript has a type called `unit` that only has one possible value, the unit value. Unit is the name of the type, AND it is the name of the single possible value of that type.

Just like how the two possible values for the boolean type (true and false) can be written with the literals `true` and `false`, the single possible value for the unit type is written with the literal `()`.

In JavaScript, calling a function that does not return any values and assigning the result to a variable will make the variable equal `undefined`. In ReScript, the result is modeled as the unit value.

Since the ReScript compiler compiles `()` to `undefined`, the unit value is `undefined` at run time.

When the computation of an expression does not yield a useful value, we can have it yield a unit value, and the entire expression will have the unit type. This is common when we are primarily evaluating an expression for its side effects.

One example of this is the `console.log` function (called `Js.log` in ReScript) – calling it returns a value of type `unit` and has the side effect of printing to the console. Any time we would want to write a function that doesn't return a value in JavaScript, the ReScript equivalent will return unit. Another example is while-loops or for-loops. Since loops do not return a value in ReScript, they evaluate to unit.

Printing and Debugging

ReScript allows us to call JavaScript's `console.log` via the `Js.log` function. This is useful for printing values and debugging our programs, and the examples in this book will make heavy use of it.

Unlike in JavaScript where `console.log` takes a variable number of arguments, ReScript's logging functions take in a fixed number of arguments. There are several different variants that we call depending on how many arguments we want to log, but they all compile to `console.log`.

Here are some examples:

`Js.log("hello")`

`Js.log2("hello", "world")` – This can be used to log two values; additionally, `log3` and `log4` can be used to log three and four things, respectively. Each argument can have a different type.

`Js.logMany(["hello", "world"])` – This can be called with an array to log many values at once, but each argument in the array must be the same type.

Bindings

Bindings in ReScript allow us to associate values with names so that they can be referenced later. They are like variable declarations in other languages, but we don't call them variables in ReScript because the value can't be changed (more on that later).

Let bindings in ReScript look similar to variable let declarations in JavaScript. Names must start with lowercase letters:

```
let x = 1
let y = 2
let z = x + y
```

Types may be added to a binding, but they are not required. If a type is added, the compiler checks to make sure that the value on the right side matches the declared type. If the type is not added, then the binding is whatever type the compiler infers the right side to have:

```
let w: unit = ()
let x: int = 1
let y: bool = true
let z: string = "hello"
```

In JavaScript, a let declaration can be updated with a new value, but we cannot declare another variable with the same name in the same scope. In ReScript, this is the exact opposite – we cannot update the binding with a new value, but we can create another binding with the same name in the same scope.

ReScript's bindings are **immutable**, meaning that their values cannot be updated, but they can be shadowed. **Shadowing** means declaring a binding with the same name as an existing one – all later usages of the name within that scope will point to the new declaration:

```
let x = 1
let x = 2
```

9

Shadowed bindings do not need to be the same type as other bindings of the same name, because they are an entirely separate declaration:

```
let x: int = 1
let x: string = "hello"
```

It's very important to emphasize that shadowing a binding is NOT the same as mutating a variable. Bindings are immutable, and shadowed bindings are in fact compiled to entirely different variables in JavaScript.

ReScript	JavaScript
`let x = Js.Math.random_int(0, 5)` `Js.log(x)`	`var x = Js_math.random_int(0, 5);` `console.log(x);`
`let x = Js.Math.random_int(0, 5)` `Js.log(x)`	`var x$1 = Js_math.random_int(0, 5);` `console.log(x$1);`
`let x = Js.Math.random_int(0, 5)` `Js.log(x)`	`var x$2 = Js_math.random_int(0, 5);` `console.log(x$2);`

Mutation and Refs

Although bindings are immutable by default, we can wrap values in a ref, allowing them to be updated without creating a new binding.

To create a ref, just wrap an expression with `ref()`. The expression will be evaluated and the result will be stored in the ref.

The ref can be bound to a name just like any other value, as shown in the following example. The type of a ref holding a value of type `'a` is `ref<'a>`:

```
let x: ref<int> = ref(0)
```

Compiler output:

```
var x = {
 contents: 0
};
```

To access the contents of a ref, use .contents:

```
let x: ref<int> = ref(0)
Js.log(x.contents)
```

Compiler output:

```
var x = {
 contents: 0
};
console.log(x.contents);
```

Console output:

```
0
```

To mutate the contents of a ref, use the := operator:

```
let x: ref<int> = ref(0)
x := x.contents + 1
Js.log(x.contents)
```

Compiler output:

```
var x = {
 contents: 0
};
x.contents = x.contents + 1 | 0;
console.log(x.contents);
```

Console output:

1

As seen in the compiled JavaScript outputs earlier, refs are essentially JavaScript objects with a single `contents` property. Be careful not to overuse refs – if we write a program that passes around a ref and mutates it in a bunch of different places, it will be difficult to track those mutations and may lead to bugs.

In general, mutation should be regarded as a feature that should be used sparingly and intentionally. In this way ReScript differs from some languages you may be used to: immutable bindings are the default and choosing to use mutation needs to be an explicit decision made by the programmer. However, there are some cases where mutation makes sense, such as when we want to write imperative loops.

Blocks

Multiple expressions can be grouped into a block, where they will be evaluated in sequence. The result of evaluating the whole block is the value of the last expression. Blocks are delimited by curly braces, and the expressions within can be separated by newlines or semicolons.

Blocks must contain at least one expression or binding, and every expression in a block *except* for the last one must evaluate to `unit`.

This expression block has type `unit` and evaluates to `unit`:

```
{
  Js.log(1); Js.log(2); Js.log(3)
}
```

This expression block has type int and evaluates to 3:

```
{
 Js.log("hello")
 3
}
```

Blocks may be used as expressions or nested in other blocks. In this example, the right-hand side of the binding is a block. Evaluating the block will print "hello" and "world" and yield the final value 3, which is what gets bound to x:

```
let x = {
 Js.log("hello")
 {
   Js.log("world")
 }
 3
}
Js.log(x)
```

Console output:

```
3
```

Unused bindings, like those that are at the end of a block, evaluate to unit:

```
let x: unit = {
 let blah = 3
}
```

Block Scoping

Bindings are local to each block.

This example prints 3, because x is only bound to the value 4 inside that block. It is also a good showcase of immutable bindings – the value of x is not updated by the new binding in the nested scope, only shadowed:

```
let x = 3
{
 let x = 4
}
Js.log(x)
```

Console output:

```
3
```

Here's an example which fails to compile, since the binding for y does not exist outside of the nested scope:

```
let x = {
 let y = Js.Math.random_int(0, 5)
 y
}
let z = y
```

Compiler output:

```
The value y can't be found
```

Conditionals

If-expressions in ReScript do not behave like if-statements in JavaScript. Instead, they are like ternaries – each branch is an expression and the entire if-expression evaluates to the value of the branch corresponding with the condition.

The semantics are pretty straightforward: if the condition evaluates to true, then only the expression in the first branch is evaluated, and if the condition evaluates to false, only the else branch is evaluated.

Here's an example of if-expressions in ReScript. They compile to ternaries in JavaScript.

ReScript	JavaScript
| ```
let x = if y > 4 {
1
} else {
2
}
``` | ```
var x = y > 4 ? 1 : 2;
``` |

If-expressions support else if syntax, which gets compiled into nested ternaries.

ReScript	JavaScript
| ```
let x = if y > 4 {
1
} else if y > 5 {
2
} else {
3
}
``` | ```
var x = y > 4 ? 1 : (
y > 5 ? 2 : 3
);
``` |

The expression in each branch of an if-expression must be the same type. Additionally, an expression must be provided for each branch, although we can omit the else branch entirely. If the else branch is not provided, the entire if-expression evaluates to unit, and every other branch must also evaluate to unit.

ReScript	JavaScript

`let x = if y > 4 {`
`()`
`}`
	`var x = (y > 4, undefined);`

Switches

Switches in ReScript are very different from switches in JavaScript or most other languages, to such an extent that I would say they are similar in name only.

Although on the surface they both let us match some expression against a number of cases and provide nice features like exhaustiveness checking, there are a number of major differences that make ReScript's switches behave differently from switches in other languages:

> Like conditionals, ReScript's switches are also expressions and will return a single value when evaluated.

> There is no fall-through in the body of each case, exactly one case will be matched, and the matching case's body will be evaluated and returned without evaluating any more cases.

> ReScript's switches can be used on complex data types.

> Cases do not have to match on literal values; they can express more complex conditions.

The last two points are very important – ReScript's switches support a powerful feature called **pattern matching**. Instead of only being able to match primitive types against literal values, conditions can be expressed as patterns, allowing cases to match complex conditions on compound data types like tuples, lists, records, etc.

As you learn about more data types in ReScript, you'll also learn how to leverage pattern matching to work with them. For now, let's see how switches can be used on the simple data types we just covered.

When used for simple data types like integers, ReScript's switches can be used similarly to JavaScript's switches. The basic syntax for a switch is outlined in the following example. Each case begins with a pipe |, then the value or pattern that we want to match against, then an arrow =>, and finally the expression that we want to evaluate and return if that case matches.

A case that is just an underscore _ is a default or wildcard which matches everything. Cases are evaluated in order, so it's common to see a wildcard case at the bottom, just like we would use a default in JavaScript switch statements:

```
let x = Js.Math.random_int(0, 5)
switch x {
| 0 => Js.log("zero")
| 1 => Js.log("one")
| _ => Js.log("some other number")
}
```

The preceding switch statement would be analogous to the following in JavaScript. Since ReScript's switch does not have fall-through cases, they can be used like JavaScript switch statements with a break at the end of each case:

```
switch x {
  case 0:
    console.log("zero");
    break;
```

```
case 1:
  console.log("one");
  break;
default:
  console.log("some other number");
}
```

Conditions *can* fall through, allowing you to use the same body and return the same value for multiple cases:

```
let x = Js.Math.random_int(0, 5)
switch x {
| 0 | 1 => Js.log("zero or one")
| _ => Js.log("some other number")
}
```

The equivalent in JavaScript would be:

```
switch x {
 case 0:
 case 1:
   console.log("zero or one");
   break;
 default:
   console.log("some other number");
}
```

Like conditionals, switches in ReScript are expressions and can be used like any other expression. For example, their result can be bound to a variable:

```
let x = Js.Math.random_int(0, 5)
let y = switch x {
| 0 | 1 => true
| _ => false
}
```

The JavaScript equivalent would be:

```
var y;
switch x {
 case 0:
 case 1:
   y = true;
   break;
 default:
   y = false;
}
```

Patterns can also be used like bindings. When we use a name instead of a literal in a pattern, it creates a binding with that name in the body of the case:

```
let x = Js.Math.random_int(0, 5)
switch x {
| y => Js.log(y)
}
```

Be careful that the binding in the case does not accidentally shadow another binding. For example, this switch statement that tries to check if x and y are equal is incorrect:

```
let x = Js.Math.random_int(0, 5)
let y = Js.Math.random_int(0, 5)
switch x {
| y => Js.log("x == y")
| _ => Js.log("x != y")
}
```

It outputs the following warnings:

`unused variable y.`

`this match case is unused.`

This is because the first case is the equivalent of adding the let y = x binding, thereby shadowing the binding for y instead of comparing against the value of y. Therefore, the first case is *always* hit, not just when x equals y.

The previous incorrect snippet is equivalent to the following:

```
let x = Js.Math.random_int(0, 5)
let y = Js.Math.random_int(0, 5)
switch x {
| _ => {
    let y = x
    Js.log("x == y")
  }
}
```

Let's go over how we would correctly write the switch from the previous example.

If we want to match against a condition that is not a literal value, we cannot include the value in the pattern directly. Instead, we can specify more complex conditions using the when clause in a case:

```
let x = Js.Math.random_int(0, 5)
let y = Js.Math.random_int(0, 5)
switch x {
| x when x == y => Js.log("x == y")
| _ => Js.log("x != y")
}
```

We can also check for conditions that are not simple equality, which is not possible using a switch in JavaScript:

```
let x = Js.Math.random_int(0, 5)
let y = Js.Math.random_int(0, 5)
switch x {
| x when x > y => Js.log("x > y")
| _ => Js.log("x <= y")
}
```

The preceding condition is equivalent to the following conditional:

```
if x > y {
    Js.log("x > y")
} else {
    Js.log("x <= y")
}
```

Loops

Loops in ReScript have different syntax to loops in JavaScript, but they have similar semantics. The body of each loop is an expression that must evaluate to unit, and the entire loop is also an expression that evaluates to unit.

For-loops in ReScript iterate between a start value and end value (both bounds are *inclusive*). We can specify whether to increment or decrement by using to or downto between the two bounds.

This is an implementation of fizz-buzz counting up to 100 in ReScript:

```
for i in 1 to 100 {
  if mod(i, 15) == 0 {
    Js.log("fizz buzz")
  } else if mod(i, 5) == 0 {
```

21

```
  Js.log("buzz")
} else if mod(i, 3) == 0 {
  Js.log("fizz")
} else {
  Js.log(i)
}
}
```

This one will do fizz-buzz in reverse order by counting down from 100:

```
for i in 100 downto 1 {
 if mod(i, 15) == 0 {
   Js.log("fizz buzz")
 } else if mod(i, 5) == 0 {
   Js.log("buzz")
 } else if mod(i, 3) == 0 {
   Js.log("fizz")
 } else {
   Js.log(i)
 }
}
```

ReScript also has while-loops, but they differ a bit from JavaScript's while-loops, thanks to immutable bindings.

For example, the following loop will run forever, because the value of x is never updated (the binding is shadowed inside the loop body):

```
let x = 5
while x > 0 {
 let x = x - 1
}
```

Mutation must be done explicitly using a ref or other mutable data type, as seen in the following example which features a loop that does terminate:

```
let x = ref(5)
while x.contents > 0 {
  x := x.contents - 1
}
```

There is no keyword to break/continue/return inside a for-loop in ReScript, but we can break out of a while-loop by updating a mutable condition:

```
let stop = ref(false)
let x = ref(5)

while !stop.contents && x.contents > 0 {
 if Js.Math.random() > 0.3 {
   stop := true
 } else {
   Js.log("Still running")
   x := x.contents - 1
 }
}
```

This is equivalent to the following in JavaScript:

```
var x = 5;
while x > 0 {
   if (Math.random() > 0.3) {
       break;
   } else {
       console.log("Still running");
       x = x - 1;
   }
}
```

This all might make ReScript's while-loops feel clunky and cumbersome compared to other languages you're used to, and some of this is because loops don't fit that well into the style of programming that ReScript encourages.

Functional programming generally seeks to reduce side effects and mutation, while loops require mutation and are evaluated purely for their side effects since they do not yield a value. ReScript makes a practical compromise here, allowing loops but requiring mutation to be explicit. Imperative loops do have a place in ReScript, but they are less important here than in other languages.

Some of the problems that we would use for-loops and while-loops to solve in JavaScript can be solved in ReScript by using recursion or higher-order functions, which you will learn about in a later chapter.

Putting It All Together

To put together some of the concepts you've learned in this chapter, let's build a simple program that takes in a year from the command line and returns whether or not it is a leap year.

To read command-line arguments from Node.js, we would normally use `process.argv`. In ReScript, we can create an external binding to access the global `process` variable like this:

```
// src/CommandLine.res

@val external process : 'a = "process"

Js.log(`Hello, ${process["argv"][2]}`)
```

Console output:

```
> node src/CommandLine.bs.js Danny
Hello, Danny
```

For our leap year program, we want to interpret the command-line argument as an integer. Arguments are represented as strings by default, but we can convert the input to an integer using the standard library:

```
// src/LeapYear.res

@val external process: 'a = "process"

let input = process["argv"][2]
let year = input->Belt.Int.fromString->Belt.Option.getExn
```

Next, we'll use a conditional expression to determine whether the year is a leap year or not:

```
let isLeapYear = if mod(year, 400) == 0 {
 true
} else if mod(year, 100) == 0 {
 false
} else if mod(year, 4) == 0 {
 true
} else {
 false
}
```

Finally, we'll print the result back to the console using string interpolation to keep things clean:

```
if isLeapYear {
 Js.log(`${input} is a leap year`)
} else {
 Js.log(`${input} is not a leap year`)
}
```

The complete program looks like this:

```
// src/LeapYear.res

@val external process: 'a = "process"

let input = process["argv"][2]
let year = input->Belt.Int.fromString->Belt.Option.getExn

let isLeapYear = if mod(year, 400) == 0 {
 true
} else if mod(year, 100) == 0 {
 false
} else if mod(year, 4) == 0 {
 true
} else {
 false
}

if isLeapYear {
 Js.log(`${input} is a leap year`)
} else {
 Js.log(`${input} is not a leap year`)
}
```

Run it and see the outputs for yourself:

```
> node src/LeapYear.bs.js 2004
2004 is a leap year

> node src/LeapYear.bs.js 2003
2003 is not a leap year
```

Final Thoughts

This chapter gives just a little taste of what ReScript offers: static typing with type inference and features that support functional programming, packaged with JavaScript-like syntax.

For readers with a JavaScript background, ReScript programs shouldn't look too different from JavaScript programs. In particular, JavaScript code that doesn't involve objects or classes should look almost identical to the equivalent in ReScript. There are semantic differences between ReScript and JavaScript that might take a while to get used to, but rest assured that this language does not force you to program in a certain way.

Although ReScript has its roots in functional programming and this book will introduce you to functional programming using ReScript, you'll find that you can still use ReScript to write programs that look and feel like JavaScript. ReScript has imperative features that you probably know and love (such as loops, arrays, and objects) while offering many nice features that JavaScript does not have, like null safety and pattern matching.

As you progress through this book, you'll learn more about functional programming and how to effectively use features found in ReScript to make your programs clean, concise, and bug-free.

In the examples from this chapter, we've already used some functions from ReScript's standard library without getting into too much detail about how they work. In the upcoming chapter, we'll dive deeper into how to define and use functions in ReScript.

CHAPTER 2

Functions

In this chapter, you will learn how to write and use functions in ReScript, and discuss topics such as recursion, pipes, and polymorphism. We'll also introduce functional programming concepts like purity and using functions as values.

Defining and Using Functions

ReScript's function definition syntax is very similar to the syntax for anonymous functions in JavaScript. The body of a function is a single expression or block, and the result of evaluating the body is the value that is returned from the function.

Here is a function that adds two numbers:

```
(x, y) => x + y
```

Here is a function with multiple lines in its body – it adds two numbers and prints the sum before returning it. Unlike in JavaScript, there is no return statement – the value returned from the function is the result of evaluating the last expression in the body:

```
(x, y) => {
 let sum = x + y
 Js.log(sum)
 sum
}
```

© Danny Yang 2023
D. Yang, *Introducing ReScript*, https://doi.org/10.1007/978-1-4842-8888-7_2

In ReScript, function definitions are values. As such, they can be bound to names using let bindings just like any other value, and they can be called using that name later.

Here's an example of declaring and calling a named function:

```
let add = (x, y) => x + y

Js.log(add(1, 2))
```

Console output:

```
3
```

In the following example, the expressions bound to a, b, and c all evaluate to 5:

```
let add = (x, y) => x + y
let a = add(2, 3)
let otherAdd = add
let b = otherAdd(2, 3)
let c = ((x, y) => x + y)(2, 3)
```

Functions can be declared anywhere, including inside other functions, and the visibility of these declarations follows the same scoping rules as other let bindings.

This means that we can define a nested helper function inside a more complex function, without making it visible outside that function. In the following example, diff is a helper function defined inside the manhattan_distance function:

```
let manhattan_distance = (x1, y1, x2, y2) => {
    let diff = (a, b) => abs(a - b)
    diff(x1, x2) + diff(y1, y2)
}
```

Nested function definitions will inherit bindings from surrounding contexts:

```
let x = 5
let func1 = y => {
 let func2 = z => {
   x + y + z
 }
 func2(5)
}

Js.log(func1(5))
```

Console output:

```
15
```

Type Annotations

Like other values in ReScript, functions have types as well. The type of a function (also called its **type signature**) consists of a list of types for each parameter, followed by the type of the value returned from the function.

Function type signatures can be expressed in the form (input1, input2, ... inputN) => output. For example, the function (x, y) => x + y is also a value of type (int, int) => int. It can only be called with **one or two** arguments of type int, and cannot be called with anything else. That is not a typo – we can call a function that has two parameters with only a single argument. More on that later!

You may have observed from the earlier examples that we don't need to annotate the function with a type, thanks to type inference. Annotations may be added if we want – input type annotations may be added after each parameter, and an output type annotation may be placed before the body of the function as follows:

```
let add = (x: int, y: int): int => x + y
```

We could also use the type signature to annotate the add binding (after all, add is just a value with type (int, int) => int), but it is a bit harder to read:

```
let add: (int, int) => int = (x, y) => x + y
```

Adding type annotations has two benefits: the first is to make the code clearer to other people who may be reading it, and the second is to add additional restrictions the possible values a function may be called with.

For example, let's say we were writing a function that checks for equality between two integers, and we want to make sure that it is only called on integers, not any other value. Without type annotations, the typechecker will infer the loosest possible restrictions on the input types – in this case, the following example may be called on any two arguments, as long as they are the same type as each other:

```
let eqInts = (a, b) => a == b
```

Adding annotations will prevent the function from being called on anything other than integers:

```
let eqInts = (a: int, b: int) => a == b
```

Using Standard Library Functions and Opening Modules

In the examples from the last chapter, you saw standard library functions like Belt.Int.toString and Belt.String.trim. The standard library is organized into modules, which are groupings of values, types, and functions. We'll go into more details about modules in a later chapter – for now, you just need to know enough to use the standard library.

Module members can be accessed using the dot notation: for example, `Belt.Int.toString` refers to the `toString` function defined inside the module called `Int`, which is nested inside the module called `Belt`.

One way to call a function in a module is to use the full name as we've seen previously:

```
let x = Belt.Int.toString(5)
```

Writing out the full name of the module can get very verbose. Luckily, we can use the open keyword to open a module and import all of its bindings into the current scope:

```
open Belt
let x = Int.toString(5)

open Belt.Int
let x = toString(5)
```

Since only the current scope is affected, you can safely use this in nested scopes or functions without it affecting any enclosing scope:

```
let x = {
 open Belt
 Int.toString(6)
}
let y = Belt.Int.toString(5)
```

Be careful when opening modules at the top level of a file – if two opened modules contain members with the same name, then the second one will shadow the first one. In this example, both `Belt` and `Js` contain nested `Int` modules. Since `Js` was opened after `Belt`, the `Int.toString` that is used in the program is the one from `Js.Int`, not `Belt.Int`:

```
open Belt
open Js

let x = Int.toString(1)
```

This code compiles and runs, but the compiler will yield the following warning:

```
[W] Line 2, column 0:
this open statement shadows the module identifier Int (which is later used)
```

```
[W] Line 1, column 0:
unused open Belt.
```

Higher-Order Functions

Since functions are values, they can also be passed as arguments into other functions. Simple functions that operate on regular data types like strings and integers and arrays are **first-order functions**, while a function that takes another function as input is called a **higher-order function**. Using higher-order functions is one aspect of functional programming called **higher-order programming**.

Many other languages, including JavaScript, also support higher-order programming – for example, the JavaScript's `Array.map` API takes in a function and applies it to every element of the original array, returning a new array with the results:

```
let arr = [1, 2, 3];
let newArr = arr.map(x => x * 2);
console.log(newArr);
```

Console output:

```
[2, 4, 6]
```

The equivalent in ReScript is the following:

```
let arr = [1, 2, 3]
let newArr = Belt.Array.map(arr, x => x * 2)
Js.log(newArr)
```

Console output:

```
[2, 4, 6]
```

One difference you'll notice between the JavaScript and ReScript examples earlier is that the JavaScript API is a method call on the array, while the ReScript API is a function that takes in the array as an input.

In fact, the concept of classes and instance methods does not exist in ReScript at all! One purpose of classes in object-oriented languages is to define data types and the permitted operations on those data types.

In ReScript, complex data types can be defined without needing a class, and modules let the programmer associate a data type with its supported operations. For example, the standard library module Js. Array2 contains functions for working with arrays.

As you learn more about the standard library, you'll probably get the feeling that using modules is a bit like using classes with only static methods, but that's not the whole picture. Modules are actually much more powerful than that, and you'll learn all about them in a later chapter.

Piping

In languages, methods and the builder pattern allow programmers to chain function calls to keep code clean:

```
let arr = [1, 2, 3];
let newArr = arr.map(x => x * 2)
                .map(x => x + 2)
                .filter(x => x > 5);
console.log(newArr);
```

Console output:

```
[6, 8]
```

In ReScript, we can chain function calls using the pipe operator. If we wanted to rewrite the previous example in ReScript, we'd probably come up with something like this:

```
let arr = [1, 2, 3]
let newArr =
 arr
 ->Js.Array2.map(x => x * 2)
 ->Js.Array2.map(x => x + 2)
 ->Js.Array2.filter(x => x > 5)
Js.log(newArr)
```

Console output:

```
[6, 8]
```

The pipe operator (->) takes the result of the expression on the left and passes it as an argument to the function on the right. The argument piped from the left corresponds to the first parameter of the function being called. Subsequent arguments are wrapped in parentheses like a regular function call.

For example, the expression arr->Js.Array2.map(x => x * 2) is equivalent to Js.Array2.map(arr, x => x * 2).

Unlike JavaScript's method chaining which is limited to the available methods of the left-hand object, ReScript's pipe operator can be used with any function as long as the types match. The next example shows that we don't even need to declare a new variable to print the array, we can pipe it directly into the Js.log function:

```
[1, 2, 3]
->Js.Array2.map(x => x * 2)
```

```
->Js.Array2.map(x => x + 2)
->Js.Array2.filter(x => x > 5)
->Js.log
```

Console output:

```
[6, 8]
```

The expression on the left of a pipe does not have to be a function call:

```
let arr = [1, 2, 3]->Js.Array2.map(x => x * 2)
```

Console output:

```
[2, 4, 6]
```

If the function on the right only has a single parameter and its argument is being piped in, then the parentheses surrounding the arguments should be omitted:

```
let double = x => x * 2
let n = 100->double->double->double
Js.log(n)
```

Console output:

```
800
```

In the following incorrect example, there is an extra set of parentheses. The expression 100->double() is equivalent to the expression double(100)() (call the double function with 100, and then call the resulting function with ()):

```
let n = 100->double()
```

Compiler output:

```
This function has type int => int
It only accepts 1 argument; here, it's called with more.
```

The pipe is a very powerful piece of syntax because it lets us compose and chain functions in a way that is easy to read.

With piping, reading the code from left to right or top to bottom matches the flow of the data, whereas nested function call expressions have to be read from inside out.

For example, writing an expression like `100->double->double->double` makes far more sense than writing something like `double(double(double(100)))`.

Since we can only pipe to the first argument in a function, functions where the first parameter is the same type as the output are easier to compose using pipes. However, not every function needs to be written to optimize for piping – only when it actually makes sense to compose functions together.

Labeled and Optional Parameters

In JavaScript, function parameters are **positional parameters** – when a function is called, the first argument corresponds to the first parameter, and the second argument to the second parameter, etc.

In addition to positional parameters, ReScript also supports **labeled parameters** (or **named parameters**). They allow arguments to be passed in any order, but each argument needs to be labeled with which parameter it's for. This is useful both for clarity and for giving us more flexibility, but it can be more verbose:

```
let labeledFun = (~arg1, ~arg2) => Js.log2(arg1, arg2)
labeledFun(~arg2=5, ~arg1=4)
```

Console output:

```
4 5
```

Labeled parameters can also be made optional by providing a default value:

```
let labeledFun = (~arg1:int=1, ~arg2=3) => Js.log2(arg1, arg2)
labeledFun()
```

Console output:

```
1 3
```

Labeling parameters is useful for making call sites clearer, but if the parameter names get too long, we can use as to make a shorter alias to refer to them with a different name inside the function body.

Any type annotations we add should come after the alias. In the following example, both very long labeled parameters use shorter aliases inside the function body, and the second parameter has a type annotation:

```
let labeledFun2 = (~veryLongParam1 as x, ~veryLongParam2 as y:
int) => {
 Js.log2(x, y)
}
labeledFun2(~veryLongParam1=10, ~veryLongParam2=10)
```

Labeled parameters may be mixed with positional parameters in any order. When a function with labeled parameters is called, the only restriction is that any positional arguments must be passed in order, while labeled arguments may be passed in any order relative to the other arguments. To illustrate this, see the following example, where the second parameter is labeled. Each function call in the example prints the same value:

```
let partiallyLabeledFun = (arg1, ~arg2, arg3, arg4) => {
 Js.log4(arg1, arg2, arg3, arg4)
}

partiallyLabeledFun(1, 3, 4, ~arg2=2)
```

```
partiallyLabeledFun(~arg2=2, 1, 3, 4)
partiallyLabeledFun(1, ~arg2=2, 3, 4)
```

Console output:

```
1 2 3 4
1 2 3 4
1 2 3 4
```

Currying and Partial Application

Currying is a feature in functional languages that allows a function to be treated as a sequence of nested functions that take a single argument each. For example, a function with two arguments is no different from a function that takes in the first argument and outputs another function, which takes in the second argument and outputs the final result.

Functions in ReScript are curried by default, which means that they support **partial application** – we can call them without providing all the arguments.

For example, the following add function can be called like a regular JavaScript function, but we can also apply one argument at a time like addCurried:

```
let add = (x, y) => x + y

let addCurried = x => (y => x + y)

// both arguments at once
add(1, 2)->Js.log

// one argument at a time
let addOne = add(1)
addOne(2)->Js.log
```

```
// equivalent to the above
let addOne = y => add(1, y)
addOne(2)->Js.log

// just like addCurried
let addCurriedOne = addCurried(1)
addCurriedOne(2)->Js.log
```

Console output:

```
3
3
3
3
```

For any function with multiple arguments, we can pass in the arguments all at once, one at a time, or anything in between. Take Js.log4, which accepts four arguments; the following function calls will all print the same result:

```
Js.log4(1, 2, 3, 4)
Js.log4(1)(2)(3)(4)
Js.log4(1)(2, 3, 4)
Js.log4(1, 2, 3)(4)
```

Console output:

```
1 2 3 4
1 2 3 4
1 2 3 4
1 2 3 4
```

It is important to note that **partially applying a function will not execute the function body**. The function body is only executed when all the arguments are applied, and a partially applied function with only one argument missing can be reused like any other function with one parameter.

Partial application is kind of neat to think about and unlocks some flexibility in how we use functions, but it should be used very sparingly. In most cases it doesn't add to expressiveness, and it has a runtime performance penalty.

Polymorphic Functions

ReScript supports **polymorphism** in functions and types. This means that type signatures are not restricted to only matching a single concrete type, and the same function can be used on multiple types of arguments. For example, we can write a function that can be called on any type of array regardless of what contents it holds.

In type signatures, polymorphic types are represented by type variables with arbitrary names prefixed with an apostrophe, like `'a`, `'b`, and `'c`.

This simple function that checks for structural equality between two values `(x, y) => x == y` has the signature `('a, 'a) => bool`. It is polymorphic because we can pass in values of any type to the function, as long as both arguments have the same type (note that both arguments in the type signature are annotated with the same type name, `'a`).

The logging function `Js.log2` has the signature `('a, 'b) => unit`. Unlike the previous example, the arguments to `Js.log2` can be different types since they have different type variables.

Polymorphism is important and useful, but you usually don't need to think about it too hard when programming. The compiler can automatically infer the types of polymorphic functions, and using polymorphic functions is the same as using regular functions.

One place where we'll encounter many polymorphic functions is the standard library for container data types. Many operations on containers like arrays are polymorphic because they do not care about the type of contents the container holds. We'll go into depth on containers and collections later, but for now we'll just look at `Belt.Array.getExn` as an example.

The `Belt.Array.getExn` function takes an array and an index, and returns the value at that index. It has the signature `(array<'a>, int) => 'a`. The name `'a` is used as a type parameter for the array type, and it's also used as the type of the returned value. This means that the type that is returned from the function is the same type as the contents of the array that the function is called with.

Another important use for polymorphism is binding to JavaScript functions, many of which are polymorphic due to JavaScript's dynamic nature. We'll discuss JavaScript bindings in more detail in a later chapter.

Pure Functions

Recall the discussion in the previous chapter about expressions and side effects – a function call is an expression, and like every other expression they evaluate to a single value and may have possible side effects. There is a concept called **purity** in functional programming which may be used to classify functions.

When a function does not depend on any external state besides its inputs and evaluating it has no side effects, then it is considered a **pure function**. Pure functions have the nice property that every time we evaluate it with the same inputs, we know it will yield the exact same results.

On the other hand, functions that have side effects or depend on external state are considered **impure functions**. A good example of this is a function that adds a row to a database and returns the number of rows in the database. That function depends on external state (the contents of the database) and also mutates that state. If we call it with the same arguments multiple times in a row, it will yield different results each time.

While it's impossible to write real-world software with only pure functions, there are good reasons to try to keep side effects under control. Pure functions are easier to reason about because their behavior is consistent, and they are easier to test as well – no need to set up external states and dependencies, just call the function with the inputs we want to test. We don't need functions to be perfectly pure, but in general the fewer side effects and dependencies on global state a function has, the easier it is to test and maintain.

In JavaScript, there's very little to stop an undisciplined programmer from writing code that has tons of side effects and is a nightmare to test. Purity is not built into ReScript either, in the sense that it's not possible to mark or infer a ReScript function as pure or impure.

In ReScript, immutability is the default and mutation generally needs to be explicit. This means there are fewer ways to interact with global state, and as you'll learn later, there are patterns of programming which can help avoid exceptions. In this way, ReScript makes it easier to keep side effects relatively minimal while still allowing the programmer to write stateful code as needed.

Although the ideas of side effects and purity aren't explicitly language features in ReScript, the reason I introduce this concept here is because it's a useful way to think about functions. Keeping this in mind going forward will help you think about software differently and write cleaner and more testable code.

Ignoring Return Values

In JavaScript, we can use any expression as a statement and ignore the value it yields – this applies to function calls as well. For example, here's a function in JavaScript that increments a counter and returns the new value:

```
let counter = 0;

let increment = () => {
    counter++;
    return counter;
}
```

If we want to increment the counter and do not care about the return value, in JavaScript we can call the `increment` function as a statement which implicitly throws away the return value:

```
increment();
increment();
increment();
console.log(increment());
```

Console output:

```
4
```

In ReScript, values have to be used or ignored explicitly. If we want to perform a computation solely for its side effects and ignore the return value, one way to do it is to pass the value to the `ignore` function, which throws away the result of the computation wrapped inside and evaluates to `()`.

Here is how we would implement the equivalent of the previous example in ReScript with `ignore`:

```
let counter = ref(0)

let increment = () => {
 counter := counter.contents + 1
 counter.contents
}

increment()->ignore
increment()->ignore
increment()->ignore
Js.log(increment())
```

Console output:

4

As shown in the example, this is useful when we are calling a function and only care about the side effects, but not the value that it returns. If we wrap a pure function with `ignore`, it effectively wastes the entire computation, because no state is changed and the returned value is thrown away.

Another way to discard returned values is to use them on the right hand side of a let binding without a name. Which one we use is up to personal preference:

```
let counter = ref(0)

let increment = () => {
 counter := counter.contents + 1
 counter.contents
}

let _ = increment()
let _ = increment()
let _ = increment()
Js.log(increment())
```

Recursion

Syntax

By default, functions in ReScript are not recursive – if we want them to be able to call themselves, they need to be explicitly marked as recursive using the keyword `rec`, like in this following example which prints a countdown:

```
let rec countdown = x => {
  Js.log(x)
  if x > 0 {
    countdown(x - 1)
  }
}
countdown(10)
```

What if we want to write two mutually recursive functions (where the first function calls the second and vice versa)?

Recall that let bindings are only visible *after* the binding is declared. If we declare the two functions with separate let bindings, the compiler will disallow cases where the first function calls the second function, because the second function's declaration is not visible to the first function:

```
let rec isEven = x => {
  if x == 0 {
    true
  } else {
    isOdd(abs(x) - 1)
  }
}

let rec isOdd = x => {
  if x == 0 {
    false
  } else {
    isEven(abs(x) - 1)
  }
}
```

Compiler output:

```
The value isOdd can't be found
```

To declare mutually recursive functions, we can declare both functions with the same let binding, separated by and. The keywords let and rec do not need to be repeated for the second declaration.

Here's the working version of the previous example:

```
let rec isEven = x => {
  if x == 0 {
      true
  } else {
      isOdd(abs(x) - 1)
  }
} and isOdd = x => {
  if x == 0 {
      false
  } else {
      isEven(abs(x) - 1)
  }
}

Js.log(isOdd(100))
Js.log(isEven(20))
```

Console output:

```
false
true
```

How to Use Recursion

Recursion is a very powerful and versatile tool in a programmer's tool belt. In ReScript, higher-order functions and recursion can help simplify logic that would otherwise need a for-loop or while-loop. Recursion is also a natural choice when traversing data types with a recursive structure, such as linked lists and trees (more on that in the next chapter).

Let's say we were writing a function to calculate the factorial of a number. If we're programming in an imperative style, we might implement it using iteration and mutable state. If we're programming in a functional style, we could implement it using recursion. I'll present four examples of the factorial function, implemented iteratively and recursively in both ReScript and JavaScript.

In JavaScript, an imperative implementation of factorial might look like this:

```
let factorial = x => {
    var result = 1
    for (var i = 1; i <= x; i++) {
        result = result * i;
    }
    return result;
}
```

The equivalent imperative implementation in ReScript looks basically identical:

```
let factorial = x => {
 let result = ref(1)
 for i in 1 to x {
   result := result.contents * i
 }
 result.contents
}
```

Here's the factorial function implemented recursively in JavaScript:

```
let factorial = x => {
```

```
    if (x == 0) {
        return 1;
    } else {
        return x * factorial(x - 1)
    }
}
```

The equivalent recursive implementation in ReScript – also virtually identical:

```
let rec factorial = x => {
  if x == 0 {
    1
  } else {
    x * factorial(x - 1)
  }
}
```

In many cases, using recursion can help us write cleaner and safer code compared to using loops and mutable state.

When expressing complex logic in a loop, we may end up tracking and updating many different variables outside the loop – collecting results, marking and checking various boolean flags, etc. With a recursive implementation, a lot of that mental overhead is eliminated – not having to worry about the state outside of the loop body means that all we need to think about are the inputs to our recursive function and what the stopping condition is.

However, there are some situations when we would want to choose loops over recursion for performance reasons. Deeply nested recursion (think thousands of recursive calls) have worse performance than loops, and in extreme cases can lead to the program crashing when it hits the call stack limit in the JavaScript runtime – try calling the isEven or isOdd example on max_int!

The ReScript compiler has a nice feature called unrolling that automatically turns some recursive functions into loops to improve performance. For example, the following recursive function does NOT compile into a recursive function in JavaScript:

```
let rec f = x => {
 if x == 0 {
   ()
 } else {
   Js.log(x)
   f(x - 1)
 }
}
```

The compiler automatically turns it into a loop for better performance:

```
function f(_x) {
 while(true) {
   var x = _x;
   if (x === 0) {
     return ;
   }
   console.log(x);
   _x = x - 1 | 0;
   continue ;
 };
}
```

It's important to emphasize that unrolling happens automatically, and it doesn't work for very complex cases. We can easily inspect the compiled output to see whether or not a recursive function was unrolled, but we cannot force the compiler to unroll a particular function. For complex and performance-sensitive computations, the only way to guarantee that our code will be compiled into a loop is to write it as a loop in the first place.

In general, the aforementioned drawbacks only come into play when writing software that is performance-sensitive or needs to handle extreme inputs. In most everyday use cases, recursion is a very useful technique for simplifying your programs.

Final Thoughts

At the syntax level, ReScript's functions should look and feel familiar to anyone with experience in JavaScript. However, ReScript offers a lot more beyond what is possible in JavaScript. Features like piping unlock a lot of flexibility in how we use functions and help keep our code clean and readable.

In this chapter we also introduced the concept of purity as a way to classify functions. While it's impossible to completely eliminate side effects from any real software application, keeping these ideas in mind can help us write code that is more self-contained and therefore easier to understand and test.

With a grasp of how functions work in ReScript, we can now begin to write more interesting programs. Until now we've mostly worked with basic data types like integers and booleans and strings. In the next few chapters, we'll discuss more complex data types built into the language, and how we can define our own custom data types.

CHAPTER 3

Composite Data Types

In this chapter, we'll discuss two composite data types fundamental to ReScript: tuples and variants.

Tuples are sequences of multiple values, while variants represent a value that can be one of several possibilities. Tuples and variants belong to a class of data types called **algebraic data types**, which allows us to model and manipulate complex data cleanly and safely.

This chapter will also cover how exceptions work in ReScript – how to throw exceptions, how to handle exceptions, and how to define custom exceptions.

Finally, we'll introduce two special types of variants that are fundamental to functional programming: options and results. Options provide null safety, while results provide a composable way to handle errors. When used correctly, they allow us to express complex operations as a logical sequence of smaller steps.

Tuples

The tuple consists of an ordered sequence of two or more values. They can be used to group and manipulate multiple values together.

© Danny Yang 2023

D. Yang, *Introducing ReScript*, https://doi.org/10.1007/978-1-4842-8888-7_3

For example, let's say we want to represent a coordinate on a 3-d plane as a collection of three integers. In JavaScript, one might represent it using an array of three numbers, but there are no guarantees that the array has the correct type and number of elements, or that the contents do not change. In contrast, ReScript's tuples are immutable, ordered, and fixed in size. This means that once a tuple is created, we are guaranteed that it always has the same number of elements, the elements are the expected types, and the contents are the same as when we first created it.

Tuples provide many type safety benefits at compile time, but at runtime they are actually the same as JavaScript arrays. This gives us the best of both worlds, because it means that tuples can be easily passed between ReScript and JavaScript code: we can pass a three-element tuple from ReScript to JavaScript code and access it like any other three-element array, or pass a three-element array from JavaScript to ReScript and use it as a tuple.

Creating Tuples

Tuples are created by putting comma-separated values in parentheses:

```
let coord = (2, 3, 4)
```

Similarly, tuple types may be declared by putting comma-separated types in parentheses:

```
type coord3d = (int, int, int)

let coord: coord3d = (2, 3, 4)

let coord2d: (int, int) = (1, 2)
```

The values in a tuple do not have to be the same type, and tuples may be nested:

```
let productInfo: (string, float) = ("celery", 2.99)
```

```
let shopper: (string, (string, float)) = ("Danny",
("carrot", 0.99))
```

Tuples can be used to return multiple values from one function:

```
let getInitialCoords = (): (int, int, int) => (0, 0, 0)
```

```
let getMinAndMax = (arr: array<int>): (int, int) => {
 let minimum = ...
 let maximum = ...
 (min, max)
}
```

Accessing Tuples

To access values inside a tuple, they must be destructured first. **Destructuring** is a way of accessing and assigning names to elements within a data type. It can be done in both let bindings and function declarations.

For example, the following binding breaks down the tuple on the right-hand side, assigning the first element to x and the second element to y:

```
let (x, y) = (1, 2)
Js.log(x)
Js.log(y)
```

Console output:

1
2

If we don't want to use every value in the tuple, we don't have to assign a name – simply use an _ in its place when destructuring:

```
let getInitialCoords = () => (0, 0)
let (x, _) = getInitialCoords()
Js.log(x)
```

Console output:

0

If the entire tuple is not bound to a name already, we can bind it to a name using the keyword as.

Destructuring	Equivalent
`let (x, y) as coord = getInitialCoords()`	`let coord = getInitialCoords()` `let (x, y) = coord`

Destructuring in a function input works similarly. Note that for the destructured example, c1 and c2 are unused bindings – they are included in the example for clarity, but normally if we do not need to use the entire tuple as a single value then we do not have to give it a name.

Destructuring	Equivalent

`let manhattanDist = ((x1, y1) as c1, (x2, y2) as c2) => {`
`abs(x1 - x2) + abs(y1 - y2)`
`}`
	`let manhattanDist =`
	`(c1, c2) => {`
	`let (x1, y1) = c1`
	`let (x2, y2) = c2`
	`abs(x1 - x2) + abs(y1 - y2)`
	`}`

Be careful when writing functions that take a single tuple as input – since function inputs are also wrapped in parentheses, it is easy to confuse a function that takes in a single tuple with a function that takes in multiple arguments.

This is a function that takes in two arguments, x and y:

```
let f = (x, y) => {
  ...
}
```

This is a function that takes in a single argument, which is a tuple with two values – notice the extra parentheses:

```
let f = ((x, y)) => {
  ...
}
```

Pattern Matching with Tuples

When pattern matching, literal values can be used inside the pattern to check for matching contents in the tuple. Just like with regular destructuring, items in the tuple can be ignored using _ in the pattern. This example returns true for tuples whose first value is 0:

```
let matchTuple1 = t => {
 switch t {
 | (0, _) => true
 | _ => false
 }
}
```

```
Js.log(matchTuple1((0, 1)))
Js.log(matchTuple1((1, 1)))
```

Console output:

```
true
false
```

We can make a single case that matches multiple literal values by separating them with |. This example returns true for tuples whose first value is 0 or 1:

```
let matchTuple2a = t => {
 switch t {
 | (0 | 1, _) => true
 | _ => false
 }
}
```

```
Js.log(matchTuple2a((0, 1)))
Js.log(matchTuple2a((1, 1)))
```

Console output:

```
true
true
```

Another way to write the preceding example would be to use multiple cases and fall-through, which is slightly more verbose but possibly easier to read:

```
let matchTuple2b = t => {
 switch t {
 | (0, _)
 | (1, _) => true
 | _ => false
 }
}
```

Destructuring can be combined with if to express more complex conditions. This example returns true for tuples whose first and second values are equal:

```
let matchTuple3 = t => {
 switch t {
 | (x, y) if x == y => true
 | _ => false
 }
}

Js.log(matchTuple3((0, 1)))
Js.log(matchTuple3((1, 1)))
```

Console output:

```
false
true
```

Pattern matching can be used to concisely express complex conditions on nested tuples. In the following example, we write a function to match any line segment that has one end at (0, 0) and has a slope of 1. Here, we represent the line with a nested tuple consisting or two pairs of integers.

```
type line2d = ((int, int), (int, int))

let matchLine = (line: line2d) => {
 switch line {
 | ((0, 0), (x, y))
 | ((x, y), (0, 0)) if x == y && x != 0 => true
 | _ => false
 }
}

matchLine(((0, 0), (1, 1)))->Js.log
matchLine(((0, 0), (0, 1)))->Js.log
matchLine(((1, 0), (1, 1)))->Js.log
```

Console output:

```
true
false
false
```

Now imagine if we had to write that in JavaScript – with all that
array indexing, the conditions are harder to read and it's easier to make
mistakes:

```
let matchLine = line => {
 return(line[0][0] == 0 && line[0][1] == 0 && line[1][0] ==
 line[1][1] && line[1][0] != 0) ||
  (line[1][0] == 0 && line[1][1] == 0 && line[0][0] == line[0]
  [1] && line[0][0] != 0)
}
```

Pattern matching is an extremely powerful tool that allows us to express conditional logic much more cleanly and concisely than we would be able to in other languages. You'll find that many of ReScript's built-in data types support pattern matching, allowing us to manipulate complex data types while keeping our code simple and readable.

Variants

Variants are used to represent values that can be exactly one of several possible types, and are known as **tagged unions** in other languages. They are the natural complement of tuples; while a tuple of (A, B) contains exactly one A and exactly one B, the variant type A | B represents something which is either A *or* B (exactly one, not both).

Declaring and Constructing Variants

Variant types are declared using a type declaration, with two or more cases separated by |. Each case consists of a capitalized name and an optional type definition for the data associated with the case.

Here are some variants we can use to represent possible colors and types of chess pieces. For these basic examples, there is no data associated with each case:

```
type color = Black | White
type pieceType = Pawn | Bishop | Knight | Rook | Queen | King
```

To create a value of a variant type, we can use the name of the case as a constructor. Since there's no data associated with our simple variants, we don't need to pass any data to their constructors:

```
let firstPlayerColor: color = White
let myKing: pieceType = King
```

Pattern Matching with Variants

Just like how enums in other languages can be used in switch statements, variants in ReScript can be used in pattern matching.

Here's a function that calculates the point value of a given type of chess piece:

```
let points = (t: pieceType) => {
 switch t {
 | Pawn => 1
 | Knight
 | Bishop => 3
 | Rook => 5
 | Queen => 9
 | King => 0
 }
}

points(Rook)->Js.log
points(Queen)->Js.log
```

Console output:

```
5
9
```

Exhaustiveness

Here's a function that returns whether a piece is a pawn or not. Notice that we don't have to list out all the other cases, since we provided a default case to handle the other types:

```
let isPawn = (t: pieceType) => {
 switch t {
```

```
  | Pawn => true
  | _ => false
  }
}

isPawn(Pawn)->Js.log
isPawn(Queen)->Js.log
```

Console output:

```
true
false
```

The benefit of representing data with variants instead of strings is that the compiler can check for exhaustiveness. Switching on a pattern will cause a compilation warning if the programmer doesn't handle all the possible cases of the variant.

For example, deleting the _ => false case in the isPawn function will result in the following warning:

```
You forgot to handle a possible case here, for example:
 Bishop | Knight | Rook | Queen | King
```

Complex Patterns

Pattern matching allows us to express complex conditions on variants and tuples concisely, because we don't need to explicitly access elements or check for equality – instead, we just provide a pattern and the compiler generates those checks for us.

In this example, we have a function that returns the rank that a chess piece of the given type and color starts in. We group t and c into a tuple before pattern matching, allowing us to check more complex conditions involving both values:

```
let startingRank = (t: pieceType, c: color) => {
 switch (t, c) {
 | (Pawn, Black) => 7
 | (_, Black) => 8
 | (Pawn, White) => 1
 | (_, White) => 0
 }
}

startingRank(Pawn, Black)->Js.log
startingRank(Rook, White)->Js.log
```

Console output:

```
7
0
```

Variants with Data

As mentioned earlier, variants are not just simple enumerations; each name can also be associated with a data type.

In the context of our chess examples, this means that not only can we define what different types of chess pieces exist, we can also associate each chess piece with its color, location, and more.

Let's define a data type to represent our chess pieces. To associate data types with a constructor, we can include the desired types in parentheses after the constructor name, separated by commas:

```
type color = Black | White
type position = (int, int)

type chessPiece =
 | Pawn(color, position, bool)
 | Knight(color, position)
```

```
| Bishop(color, position)
| Queen(color, position)
| Rook(color, position, bool)
| King(color, position, bool, bool)
```

In the preceding example, a bishop, queen, and knight store their color and current position. Pawns, kings, and rooks also store a boolean for whether or not they have been moved, and a king additionally stores another boolean representing whether or not they are currently in check.

Although the meaning of each element in the tuples are not labeled, we'll treat the king's first boolean as the "hasMoved" flag, and the second boolean as the "inCheck" flag. In the next chapter, you'll learn about data types with named fields, which are useful for ambiguous cases like this.

To create a value in our new variant type, we can call the constructor with the desired arguments. Unlike in object-oriented languages, the constructor is not actually a function, but the syntax is similar to a function call:

```
let bishop: chessPiece = Bishop(White, (1, 1))
let rook: chessPiece = Rook(White, (1, 1), false)
```

The values we pass to a constructor must match the data type expected by the variant constructor. For example, trying to construct a rook without the required boolean flag results in an error:

```
let rook: chessPiece = Rook(White, (1, 1))
```

Compiler Output:

```
This variant constructor, Rook, expects three arguments; here,
we've only found two.
```

Complex variants can still be efficiently used with pattern matching to write clean and concise code, as we'll demonstrate in the following examples.

First, we'll rewrite the points function using our new chessPiece data type. Since each constructor in our variant now has data associated with it, the patterns look a bit different. In this case we don't care about what data it contains, only the type of the piece, so we can just use an underscore in the pattern:

```
let points = (piece: chessPiece) => {
 switch piece {
 | Pawn(_) => 1
 | Knight(_)
 | Bishop(_) => 3
 | Rook(_) => 5
 | Queen(_) => 9
 | King(_) => 0
 }
}

points(Rook(White, (1, 1), false))->Js.log
points(Queen(White, (1, 4)))->Js.log
```

Console output:

```
5
9
```

In this next example, we destructure the data for each constructor in order to extract the color from a chess piece. Notice how all the cases fall through to the same result expression, because each pattern binds the color to the same name:

```
let getColor = piece => {
 switch piece {
 | Pawn(c, _, _)
 | Knight(c, _)
```

```
  | Bishop(c, _)
  | Rook(c, _, _)
  | Queen(c, _)
  | King(c, _, _, _) => c
  }
}

let whiteBishop = Bishop(White, (1,3))
let whiteKnight = Knight(White, (1,2))
let blackRook = Rook(Black, (8,1), true)
Js.log(whiteBishop->getColor === whiteKnight->getColor)
Js.log(whiteKnight->getColor === blackRook->getColor)
```

Console output:

```
true
false
```

In the next example, we have a function that returns whether an attacking piece can capture a target piece, ignoring their positions for simplicity. It returns false if the target is a king of any color, or if the target is another piece of the same color:

```
let canCapture = (attacker: chessPiece, target:
chessPiece) => {
 switch target {
 | King(_) => false
 | _ => color(attacker) !== color(target)
 }
}

let whiteBishop = Bishop(White, (1,3))
let whiteKnight = Knight(White, (2,4))
let whiteKing = King(White, (8,2), false, false)
let blackRook = Rook(Black, (8,3), false)
```

```
// can capture
Js.log(canCapture(blackRook, whiteBishop))
Js.log(canCapture(whiteKing, blackRook))

// cannot capture
Js.log(canCapture(blackRook, whiteKing))
Js.log(canCapture(whiteBishop, whiteKnight))
```

Console output:

```
true
true
false
false
```

Our final example demonstrates how powerful pattern matching can be with tuples and variants. Here, we express some of the rules for castling – a special move a player can make with their king and rook only if neither piece has moved and the king is not in check. Again, we ignore positions and obstructions to simplify the logic.

Using pattern matching, we can check conditions on both pieces at once, simultaneously making sure that the pieces are the right types, have not moved, and are not in check while also extracting the colors from both pieces to check that they are controlled by the same player:

```
let canCastle = (moving: chessPiece, target: chessPiece) => {
  switch (moving, target) {
  | (Rook(c1, _, false), King(c2, _, false, false))
  | (King(c1, _, false, false), Rook(c2, _, false)) =>
    c1 === c2
  | _ => false
  }
}
```

```
let whiteKing = King(White, (1, 5), false, false)
let whiteRook1 = Rook(White, (1, 1), false)
let whiteRook2 = Rook(White, (1, 6), true)

// this is allowed
Js.log(canCastle(whiteKing, whiteRook1))

// this is not allowed, because the rook has moved
Js.log(canCastle(whiteKing, whiteRook2))
```

Console output:

```
true
false
```

Recursive Data Types

Variants can be used to define recursive data types – data types that can be defined in terms of themselves. Examples of recursive data types include linked lists and binary trees.

A linked list is either an empty list or a node that points to another linked list (which itself is either a node or empty). A binary tree is either a leaf or a node that points to two subtrees, which themselves are either nodes or leaves.

Defining recursive variants is the same as defining a regular variant, with the addition of the rec keyword, just like for recursive functions.

Here's one way we could define a linked list using variants:

```
type rec linkedList<'a> = Node('a, linkedList<'a>) | Empty

let emptyList = Empty
let oneElement : linkedList<int> = Node(1, Empty)
let twoElements : linkedList<int> = Node(5, oneElement)
```

And here's a binary tree defined recursively using variants:

```
type rec tree<'a> = Node('a, tree<'a>, tree<'a>) | Leaf

let leaf = Leaf
let oneNode : tree<int> = Node(1, Leaf, Leaf)

// this represents the tree:
//           3
//          / \
//         2   1
let threeNodes : tree<int> = Node(3, Node(2, Leaf, Leaf),
oneNode)
```

Finally, here's a definition for booleans and some boolean expressions (&&, ||, !) using variants:

```
type rec boolExpr = True | False | And(boolExpr, boolExpr) |
Or(boolExpr, boolExpr) | Not(boolExpr)

// True && True
let expr1 = And(True, True)

// (False && True) || !True
let expr2 = Or(And(False, True), Not(True))
```

Recursive data types and recursive functions go hand in hand, because the structure of the data naturally matches the structure of the function calls. Taking advantage of this pattern lets us express computations on complex data structures in a simple and concise way.

If we think about recursive functions as a base case (where we return a value without calling the function recursively) and one or more recursive cases (where we call the function recursively), we can see how our data structure fits this pattern: in our linked list, Empty is the base case, and Node is the recursive case; in our tree, Leaf is the base case, and Node is the recursive case; in our boolean expression, True and False are the base cases, and the other constructors are recursive cases

For example, here's a function to calculate the height of a binary tree, written as a recursive function with a single switch. The Leaf case is a simple result. For the Node case, our answer depends on the height of each subtree under the node, which we can get by recursively calling the height function on the children:

```
let rec height = tree => {
 switch tree {
 | Node(_, l, r) => 1 + Js.Math.max_int(height(l), height(r))
 | Leaf => 0
 }
}

leaf->height->Js.log
oneNode->height->Js.log
threeNodes->height->Js.log
```

Console output:

```
0
1
2
```

We can also write a function to evaluate the boolean expressions we defined earlier using a recursive function with a single switch:

```
let rec compute = (expr: boolExpr): bool => {
 switch expr {
 | True => true
 | False => false
 | Not(e) => !compute(e)
 | And(e1, e2) => compute(e1) && compute(e2)
```

```
  | Or(e1, e2) => compute(e1) || compute(e2)
  }
}
```

```
expr1->compute->Js.log
expr2->compute->Js.log
```

Console output:

```
true
false
```

Options

Options are a special type of variant to represent a value that may be undefined. The option type is already built into ReScript, but it can be manually defined as follows:

```
type option<'a> = Some('a) | None
```

The Some case represents a defined value, while the None case represents an undefined value:

```
let maybeX : option<int> = Some(5)
let maybeY : option<int> = None
```

In general, any value that may be undefined is an option, and options must be unwrapped before they can be used. Options are also commonly used in functions that can fail – instead of throwing an exception they can simply return None, as in the following division example:

```
let divide = (x: int, y: int): option<int> => {
  if y === 0 {
    None
  } else {
```

```
    Some(x / y)
  }
}

divide(10, 5)->Js.log
divide(10, 0)->Js.log
```

Console output:

```
2
undefined
```

Pattern Matching Options

Unwrapping an option with pattern matching requires handling both the Some case and the None case, which guarantees that we always check and handle the case when the value is undefined:

```
let maybeX : option<int> = Some(5)
switch maybeX {
  | Some(x) => Js.log(x)
  | None => Js.log("x is undefined!")
}

let maybeY : option<int> = None
switch maybeY {
  | Some(y) => Js.log(y)
  | None => Js.log("y is undefined!")
}
```

Console output:

```
5
y is undefined!
```

Although having to unwrap optional values before using them can be hard to get used to at first, it's no more verbose (and quite a bit safer) than checking for null or undefined the old fashioned way.

The Belt.Option standard library module also provides utilities that allow us to handle options concisely. I'll highlight a few of them here.

The getWithDefault function allows us to unwrap an option into a regular value without pattern matching by providing a default value that is used if the option is None:

```
let maybeY : option<int> = None
let y : int = maybeY->Belt.Option.getWithDefault(5)

// equivalent to the following

let y : int = switch maybeY {
  | Some(y) => y
  | None => 5
}
```

The Belt.Option.map and Belt.Option.flatMap functions are higher-order functions that allow us to chain operations on options. They allow us to concisely express the logic of "apply this operation to the value only if the value is not None, otherwise return None."

As we can see from their implementation in the following, the difference between map and flatMap is that the function that map takes in returns a regular value, while the function that flatMap takes in returns an optional value:

```
let map = (opt: option<'a>, f: 'a => 'b): option<'b> => {
  switch opt {
    |Some(x) => Some(f(x))
    |None => None
  }
}
```

```
let flatMap = (opt: option<'a>, f: 'a => option<'b>):
option<'b> => {
  switch opt {
    |Some(x) => f(x)
    |None => None
  }
}
```

Since these functions both take in and return options, they can be easily composed together with piping, allowing us to define a sequence of operations on an option without ever having to pattern match!

For example, the following transform function defines a chain of operations on a string:

> Try to parse the string as an integer (this operation returns None if the string doesn't represent a valid integer).
>
> If the previous result is not None, add two.
>
> If the previous result is not None, multiply by two.
>
> If the previous result is not None, cast it back to a string.

```
open Belt

let transform = (s: string) => {
  s->Int.fromString
    ->Option.map(x => x + 2)
    ->Option.map(x => x * 2)
    ->Option.map(Int.toString)
}

let x = transform("5")
```

```
->Option.getWithDefault("x is undefined!")
->Js.log

let y = transform("asdsfdsg")

->Option.getWithDefault("y is undefined!")
->Js.log
```

Console output:

```
14
y is undefined!
```

Exceptions and Error Handling

Exceptions are a common feature in many languages, including JavaScript. As the name "exception" implies, they are normally used to represent something that went wrong during execution of a program – some operation failed, the inputs were invalid, etc.

In ReScript, the strong type system makes unexpected behaviors much less likely so exceptions should be less common than in other languages – whenever we try to use a value, we're guaranteed that it's always the type that we expect and that it's never null or undefined.

On a more philosophical level, catching exceptions is a side effect, making exceptions undesirable when programming in a purely functional style; it's often preferable to return None when the function fails and require it to be handled than to throw an exception which may or may not be handled.

That said, exceptions do exist in the language and are sometimes useful, so it's good to know how they work. In particular, there are two common types of exceptions a beginner may encounter in ReScript:

Out-of-bounds array access.

Using a standard library function that can throw – As a rule of thumb, any standard library function that can throw an exception is usually suffixed with Exn (e.g., Belt.Option.getExn).

Exceptions in ReScript are really a special type of variant, and you'll see that working with exceptions is quite similar to working with variants.

Raising Exceptions

To raise an exception, we can use **raise**. In this slightly contrived example, we have a function that takes in both 2- and 3-dimensional points and tries to extract the z-coordinate (the third value). For 2-dimensional points this third coordinate doesn't exist, so we can raise the Not_found exception here:

```
type point = Point2d(int, int) | Point3d(int, int, int)

let getZ = point => {
 switch point {
 | Point3d(_, _, z) => z
 | Point2d(_) => raise(Not_found)
 }
}
```

Catching Exceptions

Exceptions can either be caught with try/catch or handled via pattern matching.

Here's how we would catch the exception from getZ using try/catch:

```
try {
 Point2d(1, 2)->getZ->Js.log
```

```
} catch {
 | Not_found => Js.log("something went wrong!")
}
```

Notice that the catch block looks a bit like pattern matching – instead of using multiple catch blocks, we can provide cases for each type of exception we want to handle in the same catch block.

We can also add exception handling to existing pattern matching by adding an extra case for each exception we want to handle. If the expression we're matching on throws an exception while being evaluated, it will be caught by the pattern match:

```
switch Point2d(1, 2)->getZ {
| z => Js.log(z)
| exception Not_found => Js.log("something went wrong!")
}
```

Custom Exceptions

We can easily define custom exceptions using the exception keyword. These exceptions can have data associated with them, just like variants.

For example, here's a custom exception that has a string containing a message:

```
exception MyException(string)
```

As with any other variant, we can use patterns to extract the contents of the exception when it is caught:

```
let getZ = point => {
 switch point {
 | Point3d(_, _, z) => z
 | Point2d(_) => raise(MyException("expected a 3-d point!"))
```

```
  }
}
try {
 Point2d(1, 2)->getZ->Js.log
} catch {
| MyException(msg) => Js.log("caught MyException with the
following message: " ++ msg)
}
```

Console output:

```
caught MyException with the following message: expected a
3-d point!
```

If we want to throw a generic exception with a custom message, we can also just use `failwith`:

```
let getZ = point => {
 switch point {
 | Point3d(_, _, z) => z
 | Point2d(_) => failwith("expected a 3-d point!")
 }
}
```

Another Way to Handle Errors: Result

While throwing and catching exceptions might be common in other languages, this pattern has some downsides:

1. Exceptions make it harder for readers to follow the flow of a program, since a thrown exception can be caught anywhere else.

2. It's difficult to catch all the possible exceptions in the right places, and uncaught exceptions are a common source of failures in software.

3. To reduce the risk of uncaught exceptions, a programmer might misuse or overuse try/catch to swallow exceptions, but improperly swallowed exceptions leave no trace and are exceedingly difficult to debug.

4. Try/catch is not very composable, and error handling can easily get out of control and develop into pyramids of nested try/catch.

Usually, exceptions can be avoided by making possibly throwing functions return optional values instead of throwing. When accessing a map, it's much safer to return None than to throw if the key doesn't exist. This has the benefit of always forcing the user to handle the None case, making unexpected behavior impossible.

One of the downsides of using options to represent computations that can fail is that we lose the ability to differentiate between different kinds of errors. While a function can throw multiple kinds of exceptions, returning an option would return None for all those cases, making it difficult for the caller to understand what went wrong or to handle different errors appropriately.

Luckily there's a solution for that which allows us to handle errors more easily while keeping the type safety and elegance of options: the result.

The result can be defined as a variant with two cases. The Ok constructor represents a successful result, while the Error constructor represents something that went wrong:

```
type result<'a, 'b> = Ok('a) | Error('b)
```

Just like the option, the user must handle both cases for a result when they use it. The Belt.Result module provides functions for working with results, which work similarly to the functions for option:

isOk and isError check the status of the result without unpacking its contents.

getWithDefault or getExn extract an Ok result.

map and flatMap perform an operation on the value contained in the result, only if the result was Ok.

Result in Action

Let's see how results work in a real program. In the following, we have a command-line program set up similarly to our leap year program from the first chapter. This program takes in two inputs, attempts to parse them as integers, and divides them. The divide function returns a result, with the error case containing a string describing what went wrong:

```
// src/Divide.res

@val external process: 'a = "process"

let input1 = process["argv"][2]
let input2 = process["argv"][3]

let divide = (a: string, b: string): result<int, string> => {
  open Belt
  switch (Int.fromString(a), Int.fromString(b)) {
  | (Some(a_int), Some(b_int)) => if b_int == 0 {
      Error("division by zero!")
    } else {
      Ok(a_int / b_int)
    }
```

```
 | _ => Error("one of the inputs was not an integer!")
 }
}

switch divide(input1, input2) {
| Ok(n) => Js.log2("The result is:", n)
| Error(message) => Js.log2("Something went wrong:", message)
}
```

Let's run the program to see our error handling in action:

```
> node src/Divide.bs.js 10 2
The result is: 5

> node src/Divide.bs.js 10 0
Something went wrong: division by zero!

> node src/Divide.bs.js foo bar
Something went wrong: one of the inputs was not an integer!
```

Defining Errors for Results

One useful pattern when working with results define the possible types of errors with a variant, to allow for more sophisticated error handling.

Let's define the two types of errors that our division function can have:

```
type divisionError = DivideByZero | NotANumber(string)
```

Here's what our division program would look like using these new errors:

```
// src/Divide.res

type divisionError = DivideByZero | NotANumber(string)
```

```
@val external process: 'a = "process"

let input1 = process["argv"][2]
let input2 = process["argv"][3]

let divide = (a: string, b: string): result<int,
divisionError> => {
 open Belt
 switch (Int.fromString(a), Int.fromString(b)) {
 | (Some(a_int), Some(b_int)) => if b_int == 0 {
     Error(DivideByZero)
   } else {
     Ok(a_int / b_int)
   }
 | (None, _) => Error(NotANumber(a))
 | (_, None) => Error(NotANumber(b))
 }
}

switch divide(input1, input2) {
| Ok(n) => Js.log2("The result is:", n)
| Error(DivideByZero) => Js.log("division by zero!")
| Error(NotANumber(s)) => Js.log2(s, "is not a number!")
}
```

Let's run the program again:

```
> node src/Divide.bs.js 10 2
The result is: 5

> node src/Divide.bs.js 10 0
division by zero!

> node src/Divide.bs.js foo bar
foo is not a number!
```

Composing Results

Results can also easily be composed, making it easier to express programs as a sequence of operations instead of having to write nested try/catch blocks.

Let's see this in action by modifying our division program to take in a third input. Now, when running node src/Divide.bs.js a b c, the program will try to perform the operation (a / b) / c.

The program will still be structured as a pipeline – later steps only execute if all earlier steps succeeded. The final result will either be the result of all the successful steps or the first error that occurs in any step:

1. Divide the first and second numbers.

2. If the previous result is Ok, convert the result to a string (recall that the divide function accepts strings and outputs integers); otherwise, pass on the Error.

3. If the previous result is Ok, divide the result by the third number; otherwise, pass on the Error.

For step 2, we will use Belt.Result.map since Belt.Int.toString does not return a result. For the third step, we'll use Belt.Result.flatMap since the divide function returns a result. Here's what the modified program looks like:

```
// src/Divide.res

type divisionError = DivideByZero | NotANumber(string)

@val external process: 'a = "process"

let input1 = process["argv"][2]
let input2 = process["argv"][3]
let input3 = process["argv"][3]

let divide = (a: string, b: string): result<int, divisionError> => {
```

```
open Belt
switch (Int.fromString(a), Int.fromString(b)) {
| (Some(a_int), Some(b_int)) => if b_int == 0 {
    Error(DivideByZero)
  } else {
    Ok(a_int / b_int)
  }
| (None, _) => Error(NotANumber(a))
| (_, None) => Error(NotANumber(b))
}
}
```

```
open Belt
let result =
 divide(input1, input2)
 ->Result.map(n => Belt.Int.toString(n)) // if the result is a
 value, convert it back into a string
 ->Result.flatMap(n => divide(n, input3)) // if the result is a
 value, divide by the third input
```

```
switch result {
| Ok(n) => Js.log2("The result is:", n)
| Error(DivideByZero) => Js.log("division by zero!")
| Error(NotANumber(s)) => Js.log2(s, "is not a number!")
}
```

Using this pattern, any error that occurs is passed all the way to the final result, and all operations after the first failure are skipped. We can see in the following that the division by zero error from 10 / 0 occurs first and is passed to the end of the computation, and our program doesn't even try to parse bar into a number:

```
> node src/Divide.bs.js 10 0 bar
division by zero!
```

85

Final Thoughts

Composite data types like tuples and variants are very fundamental to ReScript, because they are the building blocks for more complex data types. We can define all kinds of data structures like lists, stacks, trees, and more using just tuples and variants.

The special variant types `option` and `result` are useful for writing safe and functional code using ReScript. Option allows programmers to safely work with possibly undefined values, while result provides a way to model error handling as a simple sequence of operations instead of nested try/catch.

Learning how to efficiently manipulate these data types with destructuring and pattern matching is the key to writing clean and safe code in ReScript. By now, you know enough to be able to write programs with multiple functions in ReScript, and, more importantly, to design programs that are easy to read, understand, and debug.

In the next few chapters, we'll introduce even more data types in ReScript. Some of these will sound familiar, like objects, arrays, sets, and maps. Others might be new, such as records, lists, and immutable collections.

CHAPTER 4

Records and Objects

In this chapter, we'll learn about two more composite data types: records and objects. They are useful for representing structures with named fields, and have many similarities with objects in JavaScript. We'll also discuss two different ways of thinking about types: structural and nominal typing.

Records

Records are another product type that can contain several values, similar to tuples. While tuples are a collection of ordered values, records are a collection of named values. Each record contains a number of fields with unique names each associated with a value, similar to how JavaScript objects have named properties.

Records have several important properties that differentiate them from JavaScript objects and other data types in ReScript:

Immutable by default – Unlike JavaScript objects, fields in a record are immutable by default. Updating a field will yield a new record without changing the original. However, fields may also be explicitly marked as mutable.

Nominal typing – Typechecking for records is based on the name of the type declaration, not what fields it has.

© Danny Yang 2023
D. Yang, *Introducing ReScript*, https://doi.org/10.1007/978-1-4842-8888-7_4

Nonextensible – We cannot arbitrarily add new
fields to records, and all the fields have to be defined
when the record is created.

Declaring and Creating Records

Types for records need to be declared ahead of time, and cannot be
extended. For example, here is a record that can be used to model a dog:

```
type dog = {
 name: string,
 age: int,
 owner: string,
}
```

Record literals look similar to JavaScript object literals:

```
let myDog: dog = { name: "Ruffus", age: 2, owner: "Danny" }
```

Nominal Typing

Records in ReScript use **nominal typing**, which means that records of
different named types cannot be used interchangeably, even if they have
the same fields.

When multiple record types have similar sets of fields, it is often a
good idea to explicitly label the type of record inputs or name bindings to
remove ambiguity, for both the programmer and the typechecker.

If unlabeled, the type of the record is inferred to be the type of the closest
binding. In the following example with identical dog and cat record types, if
the binding for myCat were unannotated, then the record would be inferred
to have type dog, since that is the closest matching type declaration:

```
type cat = {
 name: string,
```

```
 age: int,
 owner: string,
}

type dog = {
 name: string,
 age: int,
 owner: string,
}

let myDog = { name: "Ruffus", age: 2, owner: "Danny" }

let myCat : cat = { name: "Creamsicle", age: 13, owner:
"Danny" }
```

Accessing Record Fields

Record field accesses use the same dot notation as JavaScript object property accesses, as seen in the following example:

```
let dogYears = (dog: dog) => {
 switch dog.age {
 | 0 => 0
 | 1 => 15
 | 2 => 24
 | _ => 5 * (dog.age - 2) + 24
 }
}

Js.log(dogYears(myDog))
```

Console output:

```
24
```

Although the implementation of the function dogYears looks like it can be called on any record that has an age field, the type annotation on the parameter means it can only be called on dog type records. Even though cat type records have the exact same fields, the function cannot be called:

```
Js.log(dogYears(myCat))
```

Compiler output:

```
This has type: cat
  Somewhere wanted: dog
```

Updating Records

By default, records are immutable. This means that updating a record does not change the original; it makes a new record with the changes applied.

To create an updated record, we can use the spread operator ... in a new record literal. In the following example, the value of the age field in the original record is not changed:

```
let myDog = { name: "Ruffus", age: 2, owner: "Danny" }
let myDogOlder = {...myDog, age: 3}

Js.log(myDog.age)
Js.log(myDogOlder.age)
```

Console output:

```
2
3
```

Mutable Fields

Record fields can explicitly be marked as mutable in their type definition, which allows them to be updated in-place after initialization. In the following example, the age field is mutable:

```
type mutdog = {
    name: string,
    mutable age: int,
    owner: string,
}

let myMutableDog : mutdog = { name: "Ruffus", age: 2, owner:
"Danny" }
Js.log(myMutableDog.age)

myMutableDog.age = 3
Js.log(myMutableDog.age)
```

Console output:

```
2
3
```

Optional Fields

A record field may be marked as optional by adding ? after the field name:

```
type dogWithOptionalOwner = {
    name: string,
    age: int,
    owner?: string
}
```

When creating the record, the field may be omitted:

```
let dog1: dogWithOptionalOwner = {
    name: "Fido",
    age: 1
}

let dog2: dogWithOptionalOwner = {
    name: "Rover",
    age: 1,
    owner: "Danny"
}
```

When accessing the field at runtime, its value is an option:

```
let owner1 : option<string> = dog1.owner
let owner2 : option<string> = dog2.owner

owner1->Belt.Option.getWithDefault("no owner!")->Js.log
owner2->Belt.Option.getWithDefault("no owner!")->Js.log
```

Console output:

```
no owner!
Danny
```

Destructuring Records

Records can also be destructured in both let bindings and function declarations, allowing us to access their fields concisely.

In the following section, we'll be using this record type and declaration:

```
type dog = {
 name: string,
 age: int,
```

```
 owner: string,
}
```

```
let myDog = { name: "Ruffus", age: 2, owner: "Danny" }
```

The simplest way of destructuring records is providing a list of field names inside curly brackets.

Destructuring	Equivalent

`let {name, age, owner} = myDog`	`let name = myDog.name`
	`let age = myDog.age`
	`let owner = myDog.owner`

We do not have to include every field in this list, but field names we provide must match the field names in the record.

For example, this pattern which omits a binding for the "owner" field is allowed:

```
let {name, age} = myDog
```

This pattern which tries to bind a field that does not exist in the record is not allowed:

```
let {name, color} = myDog
```

Compiler output:

```
The record field color can't be found.
```

Similar to destructuring tuples, we can use as to bind a field to a different name. With records, we may also use a : to separate the field's original name from the new name.

Destructuring	Equivalent
`let {name as n, age as a} = myDog`	`let n = myDog.name`
`let {name: n, age: a} = myDog`	`let a = myDog.age`

This is useful in cases when we do not want our destructured field to shadow another binding, such as in the following example:

```
let name = "Danny"
let {name: dogName, age} = myDog
```

```
Js.log(`${name} has a ${Js.Int.toString(age)} year old dog
named ${dogName}`)
```

Console output:

```
"Danny has a 2 year old dog named Ruffus"
```

If we had not bound the "name" field to a different name, then the binding would have been shadowed, causing unexpected behavior:

```
let name = "Danny"
let {name, age} = myDog
```

```
Js.log(`${name} has a ${Js.Int.toString(age)} year old dog
named ${dogName}`)
```

Console output:

```
"Ruffus has a 2 year old dog named Ruffus"
```

The as keyword also allows us to simultaneously destructure a record and bind it to a name. This is useful when the record we are destructuring doesn't have a name yet (e.g., if we are destructuring a record literal or a nested record).

Destructuring	Equivalent

```let {name, age, owner} as myDogOlder = {...myDog, age: 5}```	```let myDogOlder = { name: "Ruffus", age: 2, owner: "Danny" }```
	```let name = myDogOlder.name```
	```let age = myDogOlder.age```
	```let owner = myDogOlder.owner```

All of these destructuring techniques can also be used in function declarations to destructure record inputs.

Destructuring	Equivalent

```let f = ({name}) => {```
``` ...```
```}```
	```let f = param => {```
	``` let name = param.name```
	``` ...```
	```}```

```let f = ({name} as dog) => {```
``` ...```
```}```
	```let f = dog => {```
	``` let name = dog.name```
	``` ...```
	```}```

```let f = ({name as n} as dog) => {```
``` ...```
```}```
	```let f = dog => {```
	``` let n = dog.name```
	``` ...```
	```}```

Pattern Matching with Records

Records can be pattern matched inside switches, allowing us to concisely check fields of record types. For these examples, we'll continue matching on the dog record type.

Matching against literal values looks almost like writing a record literal, except we do not have to include all the fields. This example matches any dog that has age 0:

```
let matchRecord1 = dog => {
 switch dog {
 | {age: 0} => true
 | _ => false
 }
}
```

We can match against multiple literal values separated by pipes |. This example matches any dog that has age 1 or 2:

```
let matchRecord2 = dog => {
 switch dog {
 | {age: 1 | 2} => true
 | _ => false
 }
}
```

We do not have to provide a literal value to match against, and we can destructure the record into named fields or use when to match a more complex condition. This example matches any dog whose name is the same as its owner's name:

```
let matchRecord3 = dog => {
 switch dog {
 | {name, owner} when name == owner => true
 | _ => false
 }
}
```

This example matches any dog whose name is longer than ten characters. Note that here we also bind the "name" field to n:

```
let matchRecord4 = dog => {
 switch dog {
 | {name: n} when Js.String.length(n) > 10 => true
 | _ => false
 }
}
```

The ability to pattern match on records allows us to combine them with tuples and variants to define complex data types that can be easily manipulated using pattern matching.

Records and Variants

To illustrate how to use records with variants, let's revisit the chess example from the previous chapter.

We observed that one downside of using tuples for our chess examples is the ambiguity due to the lack of labeled names. This makes it hard to tell apart two values with the same type, like the two boolean flags we defined for our king:

```
| King(color, position, bool, bool)
```

Records help solve this problem, by providing a named mapping for the fields of each piece. Redefining our chess piece variants using records gives us something like this:

```
type chessPieceRecord =
  | Pawn({color: color, pos: position, hasMoved: bool})
  | Knight({color: color, pos: position})
  | Bishop({color: color, pos: position})
  | Queen({color: color, pos: position})
```

```
  | Rook({color: color, pos: position, hasMoved: bool})
  | King({color: color, pos: position, hasMoved: bool,
    inCheck: bool})
```

Notice that the record types do not need to have separate named type declarations when used in a variant type definition.

To create a value of this new type, we can call the constructor with a record literal:

```
let rook: chessPieceRecord = Rook({color: White, pos: (1, 1),
hasMoved: false})
```

Although variants and tuples can already be pattern matched pretty efficiently, using records instead of tuples can make the code a lot more readable.

The color function no longer has to include a bunch of underscores for ignored tuple fields:

```
let color = piece => {
 switch piece {
 | Pawn({color})
 | Knight({color})
 | Bishop({color})
 | Rook({color})
 | Queen({color})
 | King({color}) => color
 }
}
```

The canCastle function can now be more explicit about each field that it is checking, making the code easier to read:

```
let canCastle = (moving: chessPieceRecord, target:
chessPieceRecord) => {
```

```
switch (moving, target) {
| (Rook({color: c1, hasMoved: false}), King({color: c2,
  hasMoved: false, inCheck: false}))
| (King({color: c1, hasMoved: false, inCheck: false}),
  Rook({color: c2, hasMoved: false})) =>
  c1 === c2
| _ => false
}
}
```

Printing Records

Since records compile to JavaScript objects at runtime, they can be easily printed using Js.log:

```
type cat = {
 name: string,
 age: int,
 owner: string,
}
```

```
let myCat : cat = { name: "Creamsicle", age: 13, owner:
"Danny" }
Js.log(myCat)
```

Console output:

```
{ "name": "Creamsicle", "age": 13, "owner": "Danny" }
```

Records and JSON

Among other uses, records can be used to model JSON payloads in our programs. Just like JSON can be parsed into objects in JavaScript, we can parse JSON into records in ReScript.

Serialization

The simplest way to serialize a record to a JSON string is to use `Js.Json.serializeExn`. As suggested by the name, it will throw at runtime if we pass a value that cannot be serialized:

```
type cat = {
 name: string,
 age: int,
 owner: string,
}
let myCat : cat = { name: "Creamsicle", age: 13, owner:
"Danny" }

let serialized = Js.Json.serializeExn(myCat)
Js.log(serialized)
```

Console output:

```
'{ "name": "Creamsicle", "age": 13, "owner": "Danny" }'
```

Deserialization

The fastest (but not necessarily the safest) way to parse a JSON string into a record is to add a custom binding to JavaScript's `JSON.parse` function.

Note that this parsing process is not type-safe and can cause unexpected errors if our JSON string does not actually match the type specified in ReScript. In a later chapter, we will cover how to validate that a JSON payload actually matches the declared types:

```
type cat = {
 name: string,
 age: int,
 owner: string,
}

// bind to JSON.parse
@scope("JSON") @val
external parseCat: string => cat = "parse"

let parsed = parseCat(`{ "name": "Creamsicle", "age": 13,
"owner": "Danny" }`)
Js.log(parsed.name)
```

Console output:

```
Creamsicle
```

Objects

Objects are another way to represent collections of named values in ReScript. They have several key properties that contrast with records:

We don't need to declare types for objects.

Objects do not support pattern matching.

Objects follow structural typing instead of nominal typing.

Compared to records, objects are harder to manipulate in ReScript, but are better for representing values passed between ReScript and JavaScript, thanks to their flexibility.

Declaring and Creating Objects

Object type declarations and literals are similar to records, except the field names are in quotes. Unlike records, we do not need to declare a named type for objects:

```
let myHamster = {"age": 1}
type hamster = {
 "age": int,
}

let myHamster : hamster = {"age" : 1}
```

We can use the fields declared in one object type as part of another object type, using the spread operator. Note that this only works for object type declarations, not for object literals:

```
type namedHamster = {
 ...hamster,
 "name": string,
}

let myHamster : namedHamster = {"age": 1, "name": "Louie"}
```

The preceding type declaration for namedHamster is equivalent to:

```
type namedHamster = {
 "age": int,
 "name": string,
}
```

Accessing Object Fields

Field accesses use the field name surrounded by quotes and square brackets. We can see this in action in the following example, which calculates the Manhattan distance from the origin on a Cartesian plane:

```
let manhattan = obj => {
  abs(obj["x"]) + abs(obj["y"])
}

Js.log(manhattan({"x": 5, "y": 6}))
```

Console output:

```
11
```

Structural Typing

Unlike records which have nominal typing, ReScript's objects have **structural typing**, which means that typechecking is based on what fields an object has.

The Manhattan function in the previous example can be called on any object as long as it has "x" and "y" fields that are both integers. The typechecker does not care about any extra fields the object has, as long as it has the fields that we need:

```
manhattan({"x": 5, "y": 10, "name": "Danny"})->Js.log
```

Console output:

```
15
```

In a way, structural typing makes ReScript's objects feel more similar to JavaScript's objects. Although JavaScript does not have static typechecking, if we wrote the equivalent Manhattan function in JavaScript, we would also be able to call it on anything that has the required x and y fields. Of course, the main difference is that ReScript's compiler prevents us from calling the function on objects that don't have the required fields, while the JavaScript implementation will just crash at runtime!

However, there are times we may want to only allow a function to be called on specific object types. This is where type declarations for objects are useful. By declaring the object's type and annotating the input, the version defined in the following can only be called on objects that match the coord type exactly, and trying to call it on anything else will cause the typechecker to complain:

```
type coord = {
  "x": int,
  "y": int,
}
let manhattan2 = (obj: coord) => {
  abs(obj["x"]) + abs(obj["y"])
}
manhattan2({"x": 5, "y": 10, "name": "Danny"})->Js.log
```

Compiler output:

```
 This has type: {"x": int, "y": int, "name": string}
Somewhere wanted: coord
The second object type has no method name
```

Mutating Objects

All objects are immutable except for objects that are imported directly from JavaScript, which can be mutated if the corresponding field in the type declaration is annotated with @set:

```
// this is raw JavaScript
%%raw("
```

```
 var foo = { x: 1 };
")
```

```
type myObj = { @set "x": int }
@val external foo: myObj = "foo"
```

```
Js.log(foo["x"])
foo["x"] = 2
Js.log(foo["x"])
```

Console output:

```
1
2
```

Printing Objects

Since ReScript objects and JavaScript objects are the same at runtime, they can be easily logged using Js.log:

```
type catObj = {
 "name": string,
 "age": int,
 "owner": string,
}
let myCat : catObj = { "name": "Creamsicle", "age": 13,
"owner": "Danny" }
Js.log(myCat)
```

Console output:

```
{ "name": "Creamsicle", "age": 13, "owner": "Danny" }
```

Objects and JSON

We can serialize and deserialize objects the same way we do with records.

Serializing Objects

Object with declared type:

```
type catObj = {
 "name": string,
 "age": int,
 "owner": string,
}
let myCat : catObj = { "name": "Creamsicle", "age": 13,
"owner": "Danny" }

let serialized = Js.Json.serializeExn(myCat)
Js.log(serialized)
```

Console output:

```
'{ "name": "Creamsicle", "age": 13, "owner": "Danny" }'
```

Object without declared type:

```
let myCat = { "name": "Creamsicle", "age": 13, "owner":
"Danny" }

let serialized = Js.Json.serializeExn(myCat)
Js.log(serialized)
```

Console output:

```
'{ "name": "Creamsicle", "age": 13, "owner": "Danny" }'
```

Deserializing Objects

Object with declared type:

```
type catObj = {
 "name": string,
 "age": int,
 "owner": string,
}

@scope("JSON") @val
external parseCat: string => catObj = "parse"

let parsed = parseCat(`{ "name": "Creamsicle", "age": 13,
"owner": "Danny" }`)
Js.log(parsed["name"])
```

Console output:

```
Creamsicle
```

When deserializing objects without a declared type, the type of the object will be inferred based on which fields are accessed and how they are used:

```
@scope("JSON") @val
external parseCat: string => 'a = "parse"

let parsed = parseCat(`{ "name": "Creamsicle", "age": 13,
"owner": "Danny" }`)
Js.log(parsed["name"])
```

Console output:

```
Creamsicle
```

Objects vs. Records

Although it would be nice to get the benefits of both records and objects in a single data type, that is impossible because we cannot have both structural and nominal typing at the same time. Therefore, as developers we must choose which one is more appropriate for our use case.

Records are a better choice for modeling complex data that we want to manipulate in ReScript thanks to their pattern matching support. On the other hand, objects can be useful for modeling simpler, read-only data and objects/functions that are imported from JavaScript.

CHAPTER 5

Lists and Arrays

ReScript has two first-class data structures that we can use to represent ordered collections of data: arrays and lists. Arrays are almost identical to JavaScript arrays, while lists are linked lists with immutable contents. In this chapter, we'll go over syntax and examples for lists and arrays, and discuss differences and use cases for each one. We'll also cover three important higher-order functions that can be used with collections: map, filter, and reduce.

Arrays

ReScript's arrays will feel very familiar to readers coming from a JavaScript background. Arrays look and feel almost exactly the same as arrays in JavaScript, and they are an important part of interoperability between ReScript and JavaScript because ReScript arrays are compiled to JavaScript arrays. This means that arrays returned from JavaScript libraries can be directly used in ReScript, and we can pass ReScript arrays directly into JavaScript functions that expect arrays as inputs.

There are two main differences between ReScript arrays and JavaScript arrays:

- ReScript arrays require all elements to be the same type.

- ReScript arrays do not have methods; instead, we can operate on arrays with standard library functions that accept the array as an argument.

Array creation, access, and update syntax are the same as JavaScript:

```
let myArray = [1, 2, 3]

let firstElt = myArray[0]

myArray[0] = 5
```

Type signatures for arrays contain the type of the array's contents surrounded by angle brackets:

```
type intArray = array<int>

let x: array<int> = [1, 2, 3]
let y: intArray = x
```

We can use generic type variables like 'a to make the type match any array:

```
let z: array<'a> = [1, 2, 3]
```

Array Standard Library

As with strings, standard library functions for arrays can be found in several places. For newcomers with a background in JavaScript, I recommend using Js.Array2 because the functions in that library correspond directly to JavaScript's array standard library. Additional functions for arrays can be found in Belt.Array.

Js.Array2 contains many common array operations, written as functions instead of methods. The functions in the two libraries I mentioned are all written "data first," meaning that the array is passed in as the first argument to the function. This allows us to take advantage of the pipe operator and chain function calls the same way we would chain method calls in JavaScript.

For example, chaining array operations in JavaScript might look something like this:

```
myArray.slice(3, 5).reverse()
```

In ReScript, it would look like this:

```
myArray->Js.Array2.slice(~start=3, ~end_=5)->Js.Array2.
reverseInPlace
```

One common imperative operation for arrays is adding an element to the end of the array. In JavaScript, this would be done using the push method:

```
myArray.push(4);
myArray.push(5);
```

In ReScript, the push function can be found in Js.Array2, but the usage is a bit different. The push operation actually returns a value, the new length of the array. In JavaScript, this is implicitly ignored by using the function call as a statement, but in ReScript the result must be explicitly ignored:

```
// using ignore
myArray->Js.Array2.push(4)->ignore
myArray->Js.Array2.push(5)->ignore

// using a binding
let _ = myArray->Js.Array2.push(4)
let _ = myArray->Js.Array2.push(5)
```

Note on Accessing Arrays

One thing to be careful of: in ReScript, the array access syntax a[b] is just shorthand for Array.get(a, b). This means that its behavior depends on the definition of Array.get in our current scope.

For example, if we define a module Array with a get function, the module definition shadows the default Array.get, and the array access syntax will no longer work:

```
module Array = {
  let get = () => ()
}

let arr = [1, 2, 3]
let x = arr[1]
```

Compiler output:

```
This function has type unit => unit
 It only accepts one argument; here, it's called with more.
```

There is one important case where this comes up – the implementation and type signature of Array.get differs between Js.Array2 and Belt.Array.

The default behavior for array accesses will throw if we try to access an index that's out-of-bounds. In contrast, the Belt standard library is designed to protect against out-of-bounds exceptions. Therefore, Belt.Array.get returns an optional value: if the index is out-of-bounds, it returns None; otherwise, it returns Some(v) where v is the value at that index.

This means that when we use open Belt in some scope, all the array accesses in that scope will need to be unwrapped explicitly.

This does not typecheck:

```
open Belt

let arr = [1, 2, 3]
let x:int = arr[1]
```

Compiler output:

```
This has type: option<int>
 Somewhere wanted: int
```

This typechecks:

```
open Belt

let arr = [1, 2, 3]
let x:int = arr[1]->Option.getWithDefault(0)
```

If desired, we can still get the "crash if out-of-bounds" behavior with the optional result by using Belt.Option.getExn:

```
open Belt

let arr = [1, 2, 3]
let x:int = arr[1]->Option.getExn
```

Higher-Order Functions for Arrays

One of the most common patterns for arrays is looping through the array to calculate some result, whether it's building up a new array or calculating a single value. Higher-order functions allow us to perform these operations on arrays without having to write loops or update variables. This makes array operations easier to write and reduces potential mistakes from mutating variables.

To illustrate what I mean, let's go over the most important higher-order functions for operating on arrays: map, filter, and reduce.

Map

Map is for situations where we want to make a new array by applying some operation to every value of the input array.

The map operation takes in two arguments:

> The **collection** – In our case, an array.

> The **mapping function** – This is a helper function that is applied to each element of the input array. The outputs of this function are stored in a new array and returned from the whole map operation.

Map is named as such because the helper function defines a mapping from the input array's values to the new array's values. The function is applied to each value individually, and the order and number of elements in the new array is the same as the original array.

For example, a diagram of the map operation to double the values of an array would look something like this:

$$[1, 2, 3, 4, 5]$$
$$\downarrow \quad \downarrow \quad \downarrow \quad \downarrow \quad \downarrow$$
$$[2, 4, 6, 8, 10]$$

The map operation for arrays exists in ReScript's standard library as `Js.Array2.map` and `Belt.Array.map`. Here's how we can use map in ReScript to double each value in an integer array. Notice that map outputs a new array – the values of the input array are unchanged:

```
let myArray = [1, 2, 3]

let doubledArray = myArray->Js.Array2.map(x => x * 2)

Js.log(myArray)
Js.log(doubledArray)
```

Console output:

```
[1, 2, 3]
[2, 4, 6]
```

If we were to write the doubling operation using a loop, it might look like this:

```
let doubledArray = []
for i in 0 to myArray->Js.Array2.length - 1 {
  doubledArray->Js.Array2.push(myArray[i] * 2)->ignore
}
```

As you can see, the version that uses higher-order functions is much cleaner – we just pass a helper function to map the value of each element, and we don't need to worry about setting up the loop or building the new array.

We can use other standard library functions as mapping functions. For example, we can trim the whitespace from an array of strings by using map with

`Js.String2.trim`:

```
let spaces = ["a     ", "   b   ", "  c"]
let noSpaces = spaces->Js.Array2.map(Js.String2.trim)
Js.log(noSpaces)
```

Console output:

```
["a", "b", "c"]
```

The signature for `Js.Array2.map` is `(array<'a>, 'a => 'b) => array<'b>`, where `'a` is the type of the input array's contents and `'b` is the type of the output array's contents.

The type of the output array is determined by the output type of the mapping function. This means that the map function does not need to return the same type as the original array. For example, the next example transforms an `array<int>` into an `array<string>` by using an `int =>` `string` function as the mapping function:

```
let stringArray = myArray->Js.Array2.map(Belt.Int.toString)
Js.log(stringArray)
```

Console output:

```
["1", "2", "3"]
```

Filter

Filter returns a new array containing only the elements of the input array that fulfill a certain condition – for example, getting only the even numbers from an array of integers.

Filter takes in two arguments:

> The **collection** – In our case, an array.

> The **predicate** – This is a helper function that gets called on each element of the array and returns a boolean. The resulting array will only include the elements of the original array for which this function returns `true`.

The condition is applied to each value individually from left to right, and the resulting array's elements are in the same order as they were in the input array.

To illustrate, here's a diagram showing how filtering only the even numbers from the array [1, 2, 3, 4, 5] would work:

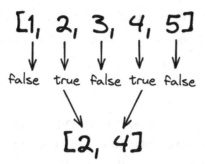

The signature for Js.Array2.filter is (array<'a>, 'a => bool) => array<'a>.

The filter operation for arrays exists in ReScript's standard library as Js.Array2.filter and Belt.Array.keep. Here's how we can use filter to get only the even numbers from an array of integers. As with map, the original array is not changed:

```
let myArray = [1, 2, 3, 4, 5]
let even = myArray->Js.Array2.filter(x => mod(x, 2) === 0)

Js.log(myArray)
Js.log(even)
```

Console output:

```
[1, 2, 3, 4, 5]
[2, 4]
```

If we were to implement filter using a for-loop, it would look like this:

```
let even = []
for i in 0 to myArray->Js.Array2.length - 1 {
 if mod(myArray[i], 2) === 0 {
   even->Js.Array2.push(myArray[i])->ignore
 }
}
```

Again, you can see that the loop version is much harder to read compared to using the higher-order filter function.

Reduce

The reduce operation is named as such because it takes a collection of values and reduces it to a single value. The resulting value can be anything – pairs, objects, even another array.

Here's an example of calculating the sum of a list of integers using reduce:

```
let myArray = [1, 2, 3]
myArray
 ->Js.Array2.reduce((sum, element) => sum + element, 0)
 ->Js.log
```

Console output:

```
6
```

The equivalent operation written using a loop would look like this – again, much less readable!

```
let currSum = ref(0)
for i in 0 to myArray->Js.Array2.length - 1 {
 let element = myArray[i]
 currSum := currSum.contents + element
}
Js.log(currSum.contents)
```

Console output:

```
6
```

Under the hood, the reduce function actually works just like the for-loop – it just handles the boilerplate of iterating through the array and tracking the accumulated value for you. Here's how:

The signature for `Js.Array2.reduce` is `(array<'a>, ('b, 'a) => 'b, 'b) => 'b`. As you can see, the reduce function takes in three arguments:

> The **collection** – In our case, the array.

> The **reducer function** – This helper function takes in the accumulator value and an element in the array, and returns a new accumulator value. It repeats this process for each element, returning the final result when it reaches the end of the array.

> The **initial value** – This is the initial value for the accumulator used when the reducer is called for the first time, or, if the collection is empty, this value is returned from the reduce operation.

Note   `Js.Array2.reduce` has a different order of arguments compared to `Belt.Array.reduce`. The former takes in the array, reducer function, and initial value in that order, while the latter takes in the initial value before the reducer function.

Let's walk through how the sum example earlier works on the array `[1, 2, 3]`:

1. The initial accumulator value is 0. The reducer function is called with the accumulator value and next element of the array (1). The result is 1.

2. The accumulator value is 1. The reducer function is called with the accumulator value and next element of the array (2). The result is 3.

3. The accumulator value is 3. The reducer function is called with the accumulator value and next element of the array (3). The result is 6 – since there are no more elements in the array, this value is returned from the reduce function.

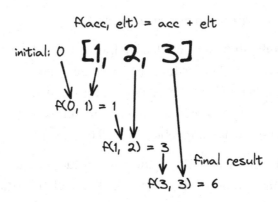

Since reduce can return any type, it is a very generic operation that can be used to implement other operations, including map and filter:

```
let map = (array, mapper) => {
 array->Js.Array2.reduce((acc, elt) => {
   acc->Js.Array2.push(mapper(elt))->ignore
   acc
 }, [])
}
```

```
let filter = (array, predicate) => {
 array->Js.Array2.reduce((acc, elt) => {
   if predicate(elt) {
     acc->Js.Array2.push(elt)->ignore
   }
   acc
 }, [])
}
```

```
[1, 2, 3]->map(x => x + 1)->Js.log
[1, 2, 3]->filter(x => x > 1)->Js.log
```

Console output:

```
[2, 3, 4]
[2, 3]
```

Here is an example of reducing down to a pair, where we use tuples and destructuring to concisely calculate the minimum and maximum values of an integer array at the same time using a single reduce operation:

```
let arr = [1, 2, 3, 4, 5]
let (min_val, max_val) = Js.Array2.reduce(
    arr,
    ((curr_min, curr_max), val) => (min(curr_min, val),
    max(curr_max, val)),
    (max_int, min_int)
)
Js.log2(min_val, max_val)
```

After seeing the previous example, you may be tempted to implement very complex operations as a single call to reduce. **Do not do this.** The point of these higher-order functions is to allow programmers to break down complex operations into smaller, more composable pieces. Grouping everything into a single reduce operation does just the opposite, increasing complexity and making code harder to read, making it just as bad (or even worse) than using a single massive loop.

Although reduce is a very general operation that *can* be used for nearly everything, that doesn't mean that it *should* be used for everything. Compared to more specialized functions like map and filter, reduce is more verbose and less readable. When a more specialized function exists, we should use that instead of reduce.

Composing Higher-Order Functions

Since map, filter, and reduce all operate on collections, they can be chained together using the pipeline operation:

```
[1, 2, 3]->Js.Array2.map(x => x * 2)
   ->Js.Array2.map(x => x + 2)
   ->Js.Array2.filter(x => x > 5)
   ->Js.Array2.reduce((a, x) => a + x, 0)
   ->Js.log
```

Console output:

14

Oftentimes, complex operations on a collection can be broken down into a series of map/filter/reduce operations that each does a single operation on the data. This keeps our code clean and organized, since now the code is just piping data through a series of simple transformations. We don't need to worry about conditions for loops or maintaining any outside state, and each simple operation in our pipeline is easy to understand and write, reducing the risk of bugs.

Higher-Order Functions in Action

To give a clearer picture of how to use higher-order functions, let's use them in a practical example. Say that we're writing software for a luggage system at an airport. Given an array of the luggage items carried by each passenger on the airplane, we want to do the following:

Calculate the baggage fee of each item.

Filter out overweight luggage items.

Return the total weight and total cost of the remaining items.

We can represent the luggage items as an array of pairs containing the owner and weight of each luggage item:

```
let luggage = [("Seth", 60), ("Sarah", 47), ("Sarah", 40),
("John", 12), ("John", 330)]
```

To calculate the fee of each luggage item, regardless of the weight, we can use Js.Array2.map to transform the array of pairs into an array of triplets with the owner's name, weight, and fee. Here, luggage items under 50lb cost $25, items from 50 to 100lb cost $50, and items >100lb cost $100:

```
let pricedLuggage = Js.Array2.map(luggage, ((owner,
weight)) => {
 let cost = if weight <= 50 {
   25
 } else if weight <= 100 {
   50
 } else {
   100
 }
 (owner, weight, cost)
})
Js.log(pricedLuggage)
```

Console output:

```
[
  [ 'Seth', 60, 50 ],
  [ 'Sarah', 47, 25 ],
  [ 'Sarah', 40, 25 ],
  [ 'John', 12, 25 ],
  [ 'John', 330, 100 ]
]
```

Next, let's filter out the overweight items. At our airport we require luggage items to be under 200lb and anything heavier gets left behind without charging the passenger. We can use Js.Array2.filter to do this:

```
let filteredLuggage = Js.Array2.filter(pricedLuggage, ((_,
weight, _)) => {
 weight <= 200
})
Js.log(filteredLuggage)
```

Console output:

```
[
 [ 'Seth', 60, 50 ],
 [ 'Sarah', 47, 25 ],
 [ 'Sarah', 40, 25 ],
 [ 'John', 12, 25 ]
]
```

Now that our luggage is priced and filtered, we can calculate the total weight and cost by using Js.Array2.reduce.

Here is the weight calculation; it simply sums up the weights in our filtered luggage array:

```
let totalWeight = Js.Array2.reduce(
 filteredLuggage,
 (total, (_, weight, _)) => {
   total + weight
 },
 0,
)
Js.log(totalWeight)
```

Console output:

```
159
```

The total cost calculation is similar:

```
let totalCost = Js.Array2.reduce(
 filteredLuggage,
 (total, (_, _, cost)) => {
   total + cost
 },
 0,
)
Js.log(totalCost)
```

Console output:

```
125
```

It's possible (and slightly more efficient) to calculate both totals at the same time by reducing to a tuple, but separating the two operations keeps our code more readable.

Let's put it all together into a single function now. All three operations can be composed using piping, allowing us to break down the logic into smaller parts like this while still being able to combine them cleanly:

```
let processLuggage = (luggage: array<(string, int)>): (int,
int) => {
 open Js.Array2

 let filteredLuggage = map(luggage, ((owner, weight)) => {
   let cost = if weight <= 50 {
     25
   } else if weight <= 100 {
     50
   } else {
```

```
    100
  }
  (owner, weight, cost)
})
->filter(((_, weight, _)) => weight <= 200)

  let totalWeight = filteredLuggage->reduce((total, (_, weight,
  _)) => {
    total + weight
  }, 0)

  let totalCost = filteredLuggage->reduce((total, (_, _,
  cost)) => {
    total + cost
  }, 0)

  (totalWeight, totalCost)
}

luggage->processLuggage->Js.log
```

Console output:

```
[159, 125]
```

Generalizing Higher-Order Functions

Higher-order functions are really flexible and can be applied in a wide variety of situations, because ultimately the behavior of map/filter/reduce is determined by the function that the caller provides. This means that a huge set of complex operations can be implemented by using some combination of these basic functions.

Here's a selection of other higher-order functions found in the `Belt.Array` library. All of these can be implemented using `reduce` or a for-loop, but they are provided in the standard library for convenience:

- `partition` – Returns a tuple of two arrays, the first one holding the values that `filter` would have returned and the second one holding the values that `filter` would have filtered out.

- `some` – Returns true if the predicate evaluates to true for any value in the array.

- `every` – Returns true if the predicate evaluates to true for every value in the array.

- `reduceReverse` – Like `reduce`, except it iterates through the array in reverse order. `myArray->reduceReverse(...)` is equivalent to `myArray->reverse->reduce(...)`. In `Belt.Array`, this is called `reduceReverse`, while in `Js.Array2` this is called `reduceRight`.

- `forEach` – This function iterates through the array and performs some operation that returns unit on each value. The entire function returns unit, so it's like a functional version of a for-loop. It's useful for performing some mutation or side effects, such as printing all the values in an array one by one.

Higher-order functions can also be generalized across different types of collections. The functions I discussed here don't just apply to arrays. As you'll see later with lists, sets, dictionaries, and more, *any* collection of values can be mapped or filtered or reduced.

Many other languages also support map, filter, and reduce in their standard libraries: arrays in JavaScript and streams in Java are just a few examples of data structures that support these operations.

Lists

ReScript's list is an immutable, singly linked list. Like other immutable data structures, there is no way to change a value in the list once it is set – instead, we can build new lists with the updates that we want to apply.

The structure of a linked list is defined recursively – every linked list is either an empty list or a node consisting of its first element (called the "head") and a pointer to the remainder of the list (called the "tail"). A one-element list is a node pointing to an empty list, a two-element list is a node pointing to a one-element list, and so on.

Building a List

Lists are constructed by wrapping the elements with `list{}`:

```
let emptyList = list{}
let myList = list{1, 2, 3}
```

Prepending an element to a list doesn't change the list; it creates a new list that's the same as the old list with an extra element in front. The syntax reflects this, where again we use the `list{}` constructor with the element we are adding followed by a spread of the list we are adding it to.

After executing the following example, y contains the values 1, 2, 3, but x still only contains the latter two values:

```
let x = list{2, 3}
let y = list{1, ...x}

x->Belt.List.toArray->Js.log
y->Belt.List.toArray->Js.log
```

Console output:

```
[2, 3]
[1, 2, 3]
```

We can prepend multiple elements to a list at the same time:

```
let z = list{0, 1, ...x}
z->Belt.List.toArray->Js.log
```

Console output:

```
[0, 1, 2, 3]
```

Immutability and Lists

One of the main benefits of using lists is that immutable updates are cheap. If we wanted to update the first element of an array without losing the previous state, we would have to copy every element of the array and then apply the change to the new array – quite an expensive operation. On the other hand, immutable updates to lists are very efficient – the operation runs in constant time because it does not need to copy any data.

The operation let newList = list{100, ...oldList} compiles to something that looks like this:

```
var newList = {
 hd: 100,
 tl: oldList,
}
```

Prepending an element to a list just creates a new node that contains the prepended value (hd) and a pointer to the rest of the list (tl). That means that newList points to a list with the new value added, while oldList still points to the list without the new value.

You might wonder: if both lists are pointed to the same objects, what if one of the lists changes – wouldn't that affect the other? The key to this is immutability. This type of cheap immutable update only works with immutable data like lists, since immutability means there is no way to change the data stored in an existing list.

Pattern Matching with List

The primary way of accessing and destructuring lists is through pattern matching. We can pattern match lists using the following basic syntax:

```
switch myList {
| list{} => Js.log("myList is empty")
| list{hd, ...tl} => Js.log("myList is not empty")
}
```

In the preceding pattern, hd is bound to the **head** (first element) of the list and tl is bound to the **tail** (rest of the list). As always, these are just arbitrary names – we could have picked other names like first and rest.

The following example shows other ways we can destructure lists in patterns:

> We can destructure more than just the first element of the list.

> Omitting the spread operator on the last part of the pattern lets us match against lists with a fixed number of elements.

```
switch myList {
| list{first, second, third, ...rest} => Js.log("this list has
at least three elements")
| list{first, second} => Js.log("this list has exactly two
elements")
| list{first, ...rest} if first > 10 =>
 Js.log("this list has at least one element and the first
element is greater than 10")
| _ => Js.log("any list that doesn't match the previous
patterns matches this")
}
```

When accessing lists with pattern matching, we always handle at least two fundamental cases: when the list is empty and when the list has at least one element. This lets us guarantee that list accesses are safe since we can only access elements that are actually there, unlike random indexing which can potentially cause an out-of-bounds exception.

Since lists are recursively structured, operating on them using recursion and pattern matching is natural. Here's an example of a recursive function that calculates the sum of a list:

```
let rec sum = list =>
 switch list {
 | list{} => 0
 | list{hd, ...tl} => hd + sum(tl)
 }

sum(list{1, 2, 3})->Js.log
```

Console output:

```
6
```

Here's a function that returns the length of a list, the equivalent of `Belt.List.length`:

```
let rec len = list =>
 switch list {
 | list{} => 0
 | list{_, ...tl} => 1 + len(tl)
 }

len(list{1, 2, 3})->Js.log
```

Console output:

```
3
```

Here's a function that checks if a list contains a certain item:

```
let rec contains = (list, item) =>
 switch list {
 | list{} => false
 | list{hd, ...tl} => hd === item || contains(tl, item)
 }

contains(list{1, 2, 3}, 0)->Js.log
contains(list{1, 2, 3}, 3)->Js.log
```

Console output:

```
false
true
```

We can unpack multiple elements in a list in a single pattern. The function in this next example returns the sum of the first two elements in the list, if the list contains at least two elements; otherwise, it returns 0:

```
let firstTwoSum = list =>
 switch list {
 | list{fst, snd, ..._} => fst + snd
 | _ => 0
 }

firstTwoSum(list{1, 2, 3})->Js.log
firstTwoSum(list{1})->Js.log
```

Console output:

```
3
0
```

We don't have to write recursive pattern matching functions every time we want to do something with a list, because the standard library provides many utilities for lists. The Belt.List standard library module supports general operations like map, keep (filter), reduce, and many more, which we can compose together to perform complex computations on lists, just like how we did with arrays.

Higher-Order Functions with Lists

While pattern matching is powerful and gives us a lot of power to implement custom logic, most of the time we don't have to use pattern matching and recursion to work with lists. Just like arrays, lists also support the higher-order functions map, keep (filter), and reduce via the Belt.List standard library. There are slight differences in naming and argument order, but aside from that usage is virtually identical to arrays.

To demonstrate, let's implement the luggage example using lists. Recall our goal was to write a processLuggage function that takes in a list of owner + weight tuples and calculates the total weight and cost of all luggage items weighing less than 200lb.

Here's our collection of luggage items again. To get a list instead of an array, we can convert it using Belt.List.fromArray (or Belt.List.toArray if we want the opposite conversion):

```
let luggage : list<(string, int)> = [
  ("Seth", 60),
  ("Sarah", 47),
  ("Sarah", 40),
  ("John", 12),
  ("John", 330)
]->Belt.List.fromArray
```

We can use Belt.List.map to transform the list of pairs to a new list of triples containing the cost of each luggage item. Again, the overweight luggage items are still present:

```
let pricedLuggage = Belt.List.map(luggage, ((owner,
weight)) => {
 let cost = if weight <= 50 {
   25
 } else if weight <= 100 {
   50
 } else {
   100
 }
 (owner, weight, cost)
})
```

```
pricedLuggage->Belt.List.toArray->Js.log
```

Console output:

```
[
 [ 'Seth', 60, 50 ],
 [ 'Sarah', 47, 25 ],
 [ 'Sarah', 40, 25 ],
 [ 'John', 12, 25 ],
 [ 'John', 330, 100 ]
]
```

We can use Belt.List.keep to filter out the overweight luggage:

```
let filteredLuggage = Belt.List.keep(pricedLuggage,
((_, weight, _)) => weight < 200)
```

```
filteredLuggage->Belt.List.toArray->Js.log
```

Console output:

```
[
  [ 'Seth', 60, 50 ],
  [ 'Sarah', 47, 25 ],
  [ 'Sarah', 40, 25 ],
  [ 'John', 12, 25 ]
]
```

We can use `Belt.List.reduce` to calculate the total weight and total cost from our list of filtered luggage in a single operation. Notice that the argument order of Belt's reduce functions is different from the argument order in `Js.Array2.reduce`:

```
let totalWeight = Belt.List.reduce(filteredLuggage, 0,
    (total, (_, weight, _)) => total + weight
)
let totalCost = Belt.List.reduce(filteredLuggage, 0,
    (total, (_, _, cost)) => total + cost
)

Js.log2(totalWeight, totalCost)
```

Console output:

```
159 125
```

Finally, we can put it all together into a single function:

```
let processLuggage = (luggage: list<(string, int)>): (int,
int) => {
 open Belt

 let filteredLuggage = List.map(luggage, ((owner, weight)) => {
   let cost = if weight <= 50 {
     25
```

```
    } else if weight <= 100 {
      50
    } else {
      100
    }
    (owner, weight, cost)
  })
  ->List.keep(((_, weight, _)) => weight < 200)

  let totalWeight = Belt.List.reduce(filteredLuggage, 0,
    (total, (_, weight, _)) => total + weight
  )
  let totalCost = Belt.List.reduce(filteredLuggage, 0,
    (total, (_, _, cost)) => total + cost
  )

  (totalWeight, totalCost)
}

luggage->processLuggage->Js.log
```

Console output:

```
[159, 125]
```

Drawbacks of Lists

Because ReScript's lists are modeled as singly linked lists, reading or
inserting at any position besides the head is inefficient because we
can only traverse the list one element at a time starting from the head.
Although there are standard library functions that let us read or update
arbitrary positions in the list, these operations are slow and expensive
compared to their array equivalents.

For example, this function inserts an item at the tail of a list, roughly equivalent to an immutable version of the array's push method:

```
let rec push = (list, item)  =>
 switch list {
 | list{} => list{item}
 | list{hd, ...tl} => list{hd, ...push(tl, item)}
 }
```

Traversing the entire list each time we add a value to the end is inefficient, especially when we have a large list or want to perform the operation many times.

Since lists compile to nested JavaScript objects, the output is less readable than arrays when printed using Js.log. When debugging or serializing data in lists, it's best to convert them to arrays using Belt.List. toArray.

Use Cases for Immutable Collections

For some readers, immutable data structures may be a relatively foreign concept. Why would we care about immutability, and what benefits does immutability bring to our programs?

Having immutability prevents errors caused by unexpected mutations. With immutable data structures like lists, once we create a list with some particular contents, we know that the original list will never change. We can pass the list around to various functions and not have to worry about those functions adding, removing, or changing elements in the list.

Immutability makes program state much easier to reason about. If we represent the state of the program with a mutable data structure, then the old state information is lost whenever the state changes, unless we explicitly make a copy of the data. Working with immutable data structures, we can easily write functions that take in a state and output a new state without changing the original. This lets us compare the old state and the new state, making it easy to validate and test state transitions or even roll back the state to the previous version.

Here's an example: say we're coding a board game, and we want to check to see if a move is legal. With an immutable state, we can create the board state after the move and validate the board, without affecting the current game state. This is also useful is in programs with multiple steps – preserving past states allows users to quickly undo commands if something goes wrong. To accomplish the same thing with a mutable state, we would need to make a deep copy of the state whenever anything changes. Doing so would be error-prone and terrible for performance, so in those situations immutability really shines.

Immutability goes hand in hand with purity – since a function that mutates any state outside of itself is considered impure, using immutable data structures makes it easier to write pure code. A function that uses or manipulates mutable external states or mutable inputs may have inconsistent behavior when called with the same input multiple times. Testing these functions would require tracking and resetting the state for each test case, and developers would need to consider much more than just the inputs of the function when making changes. On the other hand, a function that does not rely on any mutable state will always return the same thing when called with the same inputs, making it much easier to modify and test.

It's important to keep in mind that at the end of the day that immutability is not some special feature of the computer (after all, the memory of the computer is mutable); immutability is an abstraction at the programming language level. If we pass a ReScript list to a JavaScript function, the data can be mutated since it's just an object, and there is nothing stopping us from mutating objects in JavaScript. The safety and immutability guarantees are a feature of the language and type system that we're using.

Lists vs. Arrays

When should I use an array and when should I use a list? Arrays are more generally useful and versatile, while lists are less flexible but provide additional safety guarantees through pattern matching and immutability.

For a lot of common use cases like iterating through a collection or performing common operations like map and filter, either data structure can be used.

You should probably use arrays if

- There will be a lot of elements, and performance is a concern.

- You want to read/update/add elements at arbitrary positions.

- The data will be passed between JavaScript and ReScript code.

You should probably use lists if

- You want immutability, or your data is read-only.

- You want better pattern matching and type safety.

- Your data will only be used within ReScript code.

If your program's requirements do not fit cleanly in one category, it is also possible to convert between lists and arrays, but there is a performance cost if this is done too frequently.

Final Thoughts

While ReScript's lists may seem like a strange data structure, they are very powerful because they offer immutable collections built into the language. With their recursive structure, they are a natural fit for ReScript's powerful pattern matching, allowing us to write cleaner and more elegant code than we could with arrays.

The choice of using lists or arrays ultimately comes down to how we want to write our programs. If we want to write code in a more functional style and want the benefits of immutability, lists are the natural choice. If we want our code to look and feel more like JavaScript, then arrays are the better choice.

In the next chapter, we'll discuss other collections in ReScript's standard libraries: sets, maps, stacks, and queues.

CHAPTER 6

Collections

In this chapter, we'll discuss other common data structures for representing collections of values: sets, maps, stacks, and queues. ReScript's standard libraries provide several options for these collections, with similar APIs but different use cases. We'll break down these collections into two categories: immutable collections and mutable collections.

Like lists, updates on immutable collections are functional and do not actually change the contents of the collection being updated. Instead, they return a new collection with the update applied.

The immutable collections we will cover include Belt.Set and Belt.Map.

Like arrays, updates on mutable collections change the contents of the collection. They are similar to collections in JavaScript.

The mutable collections we will cover include

Belt.HashSet

Belt.MutableSet

Belt.MutableMap

Belt.HashMap

Js.Dict

Belt.MutableQueue

Belt.MutableStack

© Danny Yang 2023
D. Yang, *Introducing ReScript*, https://doi.org/10.1007/978-1-4842-8888-7_6

For reference, here are some tables comparing different types of sets and maps in ReScript's standard library. We'll go into more detail about their usage and performance later in the chapter, and it may be useful to refer back to this table for side-by-side comparisons.

First, let's compare the three different types of sets:

Collection	Mutable?	Can store anything?	Performance	Runtime Representation
Belt.Set	immutable	yes, with custom comparator	logarithmic	tree
Belt.MutableSet	mutable	yes, with custom comparator	logarithmic	tree
Belt.HashSet	mutable	yes, with custom hash function	constant	hash table

Next, let's look at the four different types of maps:

Collection	Mutable?	JSON-compatible?	Keys can be anything?	Performance	Runtime Representation
Belt.Map	immutable	no	yes, with custom comparator	logarithmic	tree
Belt.MutableMap	mutable	no	yes, with custom comparator	logarithmic	tree
Belt.HashMap	mutable	no	yes, with custom hash function	constant	hash table
Js.Dict	mutable	yes	no, string keys only	constant	JavaScript object

Immutable Collections

ReScript's standard library supports immutable sets and maps, through the `Belt.Set` and `Belt.Map` modules.

Similar to lists, updates made to these immutable collections do not modify the original collection. Unlike lists however, random lookups have good performance – the time to look up a certain value in an immutable set/map scales logarithmically with the number of elements it has.

Another useful property of these immutable collections is that they are naturally sorted. This means that operations that iterate through all the keys, such as map, forEach, reduce, etc., will iterate through the keys in a predictable order, and finding the minimum/maximum key in the collection costs the same as looking up any other key.

Immutable Sets

Belt.Set is an immutable collection used to store a set of unique values.

There are two specialized submodules to support common use cases: use Belt.Set.Int for sets of integers and Belt.Set.String for sets of strings.

Creating a Set

Sets can be initialized empty or from an array of values:

```
open Belt

let emptySet = Set.String.empty

let birdSet = Set.String.fromArray([
    "robin",
    "robin",
    "sparrow",
    "duck"
])
```

Sets can be easily converted to arrays and lists with toArray and toList, respectively. The former is also useful for debugging purposes, since arrays have a more readable format when printed:

```
birdSet->Set.String.toArray->Js.log
```

Console output:

```
["duck", "robin", "sparrow"]
```

Updating a Set

Updating a set returns a new set without modifying the original:

```
let set = Set.String.empty
let set' = set->Set.String.add("duck")
let set'' = set'->Set.String.remove("duck")

Js.log(Set.String.size(set))
Js.log(Set.String.size(set'))
Js.log(Set.String.size(set''))
```

Console output:

```
0
1
0
```

Updates and operations can be chained using the pipe operator:

```
let set = Set.String.empty
 ->Set.String.add("duck")
 ->Set.String.add("pigeon")
 ->Set.String.add("duck")
 ->Set.String.remove("pigeon")

set->Set.String.toArray->Js.log
```

Console output:

```
["duck"]
```

Common Set Operations

Use Set.has to check if an element is in a set:

```
let seenBirds = Set.String.fromArray(["duck"])
let hasSeenDuck = Set.String.has(set, "duck")
let hasSeenChicken = Set.String.has(set, "chicken")

Js.log(hasSeenDuck)
Js.log(hasSeenChicken)
```

Console output:

```
true
false
```

The API for sets supports common operations such as union (union), intersection (intersect), and difference (diff). These operations will all return a new set without changing the inputs:

```
let allSeenBirds = Set.String.union(seenBirdsDay1,
seenBirdsDay2)
let seenBothDays = Set.String.intersect(seenBirdsDay1,
seenBirdsDay2)
let seenFirstDayOnly = Set.String.diff(seenBirdsDay1,
seenBirdsDay2)

allSeenBirds->Set.String.toArray->Js.log
seenBothDays->Set.String.toArray->Js.log
seenFirstDayOnly->Set.String.toArray->Js.log
```

Console output:

```
["duck", "pelican", "robin", "sparrow"]
["duck"]
["robin", "sparrow"]
```

Immutable Maps

Belt.Map is an immutable collection used to store key-value mappings. The interface for maps is very similar to the interface for sets. Use Belt. Map.Int for maps with integer keys, and Belt.Map.String for maps with string keys.

Here are some examples showing how to use Belt.Map.String. Maps with other key types work the same way; the main difference is which module's functions are being used.

Creating a Map

Maps can be initialized empty or from an array or list of key-value pairs:

```
open Belt

let emptyMap = Map.String.empty

let birdCount = Map.String.fromArray([
    ("duck", 126),
    ("goose", 23),
    ("pelican", 3),
    ("heron", 5)
])
```

Maps may be converted to an array of key-value pairs using toArray. This is useful if we need to print the contents of the map:

```
birdCount->Map.String.toArray->Js.log
```

Console output:

```
[
 ["duck", 126],
 ["goose", 23],
 ["heron", 5],
 ["pelican", 3]
]
```

Updating a Map

Map updates are immutable, meaning they return a new map without modifying the original:

```
let map = Map.String.empty
let map' = map->Map.String.set("duck", 10)
let map'' = map'->Map.String.remove("duck")

map->Map.String.size->Js.log
map'->Map.String.size->Js.log
map''->Map.String.size->Js.log
```

Console output:

```
0
1
0
```

As with sets, updates and other operations can be chained using the pipe operator:

```
let map = Map.String.empty
 ->Map.String.set("duck", 10)
 ->Map.String.set("pigeon", 5)
 ->Map.String.remove("pigeon")

map->Map.String.toArray->Js.log
```

Console output:

```
[["duck", 10]]
```

Accessing a Map

There are three APIs that can be used to access values in maps:

get returns an optional value, forcing us to handle cases when the key does not exist.

getExn throws Not_found if the key does not exist.

getWithDefault returns a default value if the key does not exist.

Here are some examples of those APIs in action:

```
let sawPelicans = Map.String.get(birdCount, "pelican")
switch sawPelicans {
| Some(_) => Js.log("saw pelicans")
| None => Js.log("did not see pelicans")
}

let ducks = Map.String.getExn(birdCount, "duck")
Js.log(ducks)

let swans = Map.String.getWithDefault(birdCount, "swan", 0)
Js.log(swans)
```

Console output:

```
saw pelicans
126
0
```

Using Collections: Luggage Example Revisited

One common use case for collections is aggregating values from a list or array. Recall the luggage example from the last chapter, where we had the following array of passengers and their luggage:

```
let luggage = [("Seth", 60), ("Sarah", 47), ("Sarah", 40),
("John", 12), ("John", 330)]
```

To get the set of passenger names without duplicates, we can use a set. First, we use Array.map to get an array of just the names. Then, we create a set. Finally, we convert the set back into a new array without duplicates:

```
let passengers = Belt.Array.map(luggage, ((name, _)) => name)
 ->Belt.Set.String.fromArray
 ->Belt.Set.String.toArray
Js.log(passengers)
```

Console output:

```
["John", "Sarah", "Seth"]
```

Recall that in the previous chapter we also wanted to calculate the total weight of the luggage carried by each passenger. That can be done easily and cleanly using a map.

We start with an empty map and use Array.reduce with an accumulator function that returns the updated map at each step. Notice that using getWithDefault allows us to avoid having to specify separate cases to handle whether or not the key already exists:

```
let totalLuggagePerPerson = (luggage: array<(string, int)>) => {
 open Belt
 Array.reduce(luggage, Map.String.empty, (weights, (person,
 weight)) => {
   let curr = weights->Map.String.getWithDefault(person, 0)
```

```
  weights->Map.String.set(person, curr + weight)
 })
}
```

```
luggage->totalLuggagePerPerson->Map.String.toArray->Js.log
```

Console output:

```
[
 ["John", 342],
 ["Sarah", 87],
 ["Seth", 60]
]
```

Higher-order functions like map, keep, and reduce are not just for lists and arrays; they can be used on standard library collections as well:

```
let luggageMap = totalLuggagePerPerson(luggage)
```

```
let tooMuchLuggage = luggageMap->Belt.Map.String.keep((_,
weight) => weight > 200)
tooMuchLuggage->Map.String.keysToArray->Js.log
```

```
let totalLuggageWeight = luggageMap->Belt.Map.String.reduce(0,
   (sum, _, weight) => sum + weight
)
Js.log(totalLuggageWeight)
```

Console output:

```
["John"]
489
```

Advanced Topic: Generic Collections

While working with collections, we're bound to come across cases where we want to use custom data types (not strings or integers) in our collection.

Unlike many other languages, ReScript allows us to use complex data like arrays or objects as the keys for sets and maps. There isn't really a distinction between "primitives" and "references/objects" – all data types are treated equally and a generic set or map can hold anything, as long as there's a way to compare them.

The first step to creating a generic set is defining a comparison function for our data type. The comparison function takes in two values, returning -1 if the first value is "less" than the second value, 1 if the first value is "greater" than the second value, and 0 if the values are the "same." How we define "less," "greater," and "same" are entirely up to us, as long as the definitions are consistent. The reason we need to define these comparisons is because values in a set and keys in a map are ordered, and we need a way to define a global ordering over the possible values in the set.

To illustrate, let's define a comparison function for integers (creating a set with this would be roughly equivalent to `Belt.Set.Int`):

```
module IntCmp = Belt.Id.MakeComparable({
  type t = int
  let cmp = (a, b) => {
    if a < b {
      -1
    } else if a > b {
      1
    } else {
      0
    }
  }
})
```

Notice that we're actually calling Belt.Id.MakeComparable on a module that contains the definitions of our data type and comparison function. The idea of functions that take in modules and create other modules is called **functor** – we'll explore that in more detail in a later chapter.

With our custom comparable module defined, we can create generic sets by passing our comparable module in the ~id named parameter. In the example we initialize the set from an array using Set.fromArray; empty sets can be created using Set.make:

```
let intSet = Belt.Set.fromArray([1, 2, 3, 4, 4],
~id=module(IntCmp))
intSet->Belt.Set.toArray->Js.log
```

Console output:

```
[1, 2, 3, 4]
```

If we want the values in the set to be in reverse order, we can simply change the comparison function:

```
module RevIntCmp = Belt.Id.MakeComparable({
 type t = int
 let cmp = (a, b) => {
   if a < b {
     1
   } else if a > b {
     -1
   } else {
     0
   }
 }
})
```

```
let revIntSet = Belt.Set.fromArray([1, 2, 3, 4, 4],
~id=module(RevIntCmp))
revIntSet->Belt.Set.toArray->Js.log
```

Console output:

```
[4, 3, 2, 1]
```

Now that we've covered how to define custom comparables, let's apply this to a more practical example – the board game Battleship. Battleship involves two players trying to sink each other's ships placed on separate 10x10 grids. Players take turns guessing coordinates on the grid without knowing where the other player's ships are – if the guessed coordinate has a ship on it, then that ship is "hit."

In our Battleship game, coordinates are tuples of two integers representing the x and y values, respectively. We can use sets of coordinates to represent the locations that have already been guessed, and the locations of the ships. To create a generic set of coordinates, we need to first define a comparable module:

```
module CoordCmp = Belt.Id.MakeComparable({
  type t = (int, int)
  let cmp = (a, b) => Pervasives.compare(a, b)
})
```

Custom Comparison Functions

We used Pervasives.compare to define the comparison function. This is sort of a generic deep comparison function that we can use for composite data types like tuples. It's handy, but may be less efficient than a manually defined comparison function. If we wanted to implement the comparison function for integer pairs manually, it might look something like this:

```
let cmp = ((x1, y1), (x2, y2)) => {
 if x1 < x2 {
   -1
 } else if x1 > x2 {
   1
 } else if y1 < y2 {
   -1
 } else if y1 > y2 {
   1
 } else {
   0
 }
}
```

Next, we'll initialize a set of coordinates we have already guessed, along with a set of coordinates that contain a ship:

```
let guessed = Belt.Set.fromArray([(1,1)], ~id=module(CoordCmp))
let ships = Belt.Set.fromArray([(2,2), (2,3), (2,4)],
~id=module(CoordCmp))
```

Finally, we'll write a function that checks a coordinate value against the contents of the sets and print out an appropriate message for the player. For simplicity, we'll treat out-of-bounds shots as misses.

Notice that we do not have to pass the ~id param to any of the generic set functions after we create it:

```
let checkCoord = ((x, y) as coord, guesses, ships) => {
 open Belt
 if guesses->Set.has(coord) {
   Js.log("already guessed")
 } else if ships->Set.has(coord) {
   Js.log("hit")
```

```
  } else {
    Js.log("miss")
  }
}

checkCoord((1, 1), guessed, ships)
checkCoord((0, 0), guessed, ships)
checkCoord((2, 2), guessed, ships)
```

Console output:

```
already guessed
miss
hit
```

We can use the same method to create maps with generic keys. To give a more concrete example, let's reimplement what we have from before using a generic map. This time, we will create a map where the keys are x-y coordinates and the values are what is on those coordinates. Again, we will ignore out-of-bounds checks and omit empty squares for simplicity.

First, we'll define a simple variant type for the values:

```
type grid = Ship | Guessed
```

Next, we'll initialize a generic map with some initial values like we did with sets earlier:

```
let board = Belt.Map.fromArray(
  [((2, 2), Ship), ((2, 3), Ship), ((2, 4), Ship), ((1, 1),
  Guessed)],
  ~id=module(CoordCmp),
)
```

Finally, we can use switch to pattern match on the optional value returned from Map.get to elegantly implement checkCoord:

```
let checkCoord = ((x, y) as coord, board) => {
 switch Belt.Map.get(board, coord) {
 | Some(Guessed) => Js.log("already guessed")
 | Some(Ship) => Js.log("hit")
 | None => Js.log("miss")
 }
}

checkCoord((1, 1), board)
checkCoord((0, 0), board)
checkCoord((2, 2), board)
```

Console output:

```
already guessed
miss
hit
```

Mutable Collections

In addition to immutable collections, ReScript's standard library also supports a number of mutable collections. These mutable collections work the same way that arrays and collections work in JavaScript – any updates will mutate the collection in-place.

Mutable collections are useful even if we are writing code in a functional style, and in some cases it is preferable to use mutable collections over immutable ones for reasons such as performance or JSON compatibility. In addition to mutable versions of map and set, ReScript's standard library also offers mutable stacks and queues.

Mutable Stack

`Belt.MutableStack` implements a LIFO (last-in first-out) stack data structure. As its name suggests, updates to the stack modify it in place. A mutable stack can contain elements of any type, as long as its contents are all the same type.

Empty stacks are created using the make function, and elements can be added using push:

```
open Belt

let s = MutableStack.make()

s->MutableStack.push("a")
s->MutableStack.push("b")
s->MutableStack.push("c")
```

The pop function mutates the stack to remove the top element and returns the element. The top function returns the top element without removing it from the stack. Both of these functions return optional values – if the stack is not empty, then they will return the element wrapped with Some; otherwise, they will return None:

```
let s = MutableStack.make()

s->MutableStack.push("a")
s->MutableStack.push("b")
s->MutableStack.push("c")

s->MutableStack.size->Js.log
s->MutableStack.pop->Option.getExn->Js.log
s->MutableStack.size->Js.log
s->MutableStack.top->Option.getExn->Js.log
s->MutableStack.size->Js.log
```

Console output:

3
c
2
b
2

We can iterate through the elements of a stack using the forEach function. The iteration order will always be the same order elements would be popped in, the reverse of the insertion order:

```
let s = MutableStack.make()

s->MutableStack.push("a")
s->MutableStack.push("b")
s->MutableStack.push("c")

s->MutableStack.forEach(Js.log)
```

Console output:

c
b
a

This is just one possible implementation of a stack in ReScript, and by no means are we forced to use it. There are also other alternatives to this module if we want a stack with different properties:

> If we want an *immutable* stack, we can just use a list and push/pop values from the head.

> If we want a stack that is printable/JSON-serializable and interoperable with JavaScript code, we can just use an array and push/pop values from one end.

Mutable Queue

MutableQueue implements a FIFO (first-in first-out) queue data structure. Like MutableStack, updates will mutate the queue in place.

Queues can be initialized empty using make, or initialized from an array using fromArray. The elements in the array will be added to the queue in order. Elements can be added to the queue using add:

```
open Belt

let q = MutableQueue.make()
let q2 = MutableQueue.fromArray([1, 2, 3, 4, 5])

q->MutableQueue.size->Js.log
q2->MutableQueue.size->Js.log

q->MutableQueue.add(1)
q->MutableQueue.size->Js.log
```

Console output:

```
0
5
1
```

The pop function mutates the queue to remove the first element and returns the element. The peek function returns the first element without removing it from the queue. Similar to mutable stack both of these functions return optional values, although MutableQueue also provides the popExn and peekExn functions, which return unwrapped values but will throw if the queue is empty.

```
let q = MutableQueue.make()

q->MutableQueue.add("a")
q->MutableQueue.add("b")
```

159

```
q->MutableQueue.add("c")

q->MutableQueue.size->Js.log
q->MutableQueue.popExn->Js.log
q->MutableQueue.size->Js.log
q->MutableQueue.peekExn->Js.log
q->MutableQueue.size->Js.log
```

Console output:

```
3
a
2
b
2
```

The toArray function can be used to convert queues into arrays. The first element in the queue will always be at the beginning of the array, and the last element of the queue will always be at the end of the array:

```
let q = MutableQueue.make()
q->MutableQueue.add("a")
q->MutableQueue.add("b")
q->MutableQueue.add("c")

q->MutableQueue.toArray->Js.log
```

Console output:

```
["a", "b", "c"]
```

This is useful when we want to print/serialize the contents of the queue, or if we want to use the array standard library to manipulate the contents of the queue. MutableQueue supports operations like forEach, map, and reduce, but the array standard library contains a wider selection.

Mutable Set and Mutable Map

As their name suggests, Belt.MutableSet and Belt.MutableMap are mutable versions of the Belt.Set and Belt.Map modules described earlier in the chapter. Their performance characteristics are very similar – updates and accesses scale logarithmically with the number of elements in the collection.

We can use MutableSet and MutableMap with generic types using a custom comparable module, just like we would for the immutable Set/Map.

The basic APIs of MutableSet/MutableMap are almost identical to those of Set/Map, with the main difference being that update operations modify the collection in place and return unit, instead of returning an updated collection.

Mutable Map Example

To illustrate this difference, we can revisit the luggage example again using a MutableMap. Here, we use Array.forEach to build the map – since updates happen in place, we do not need to pass along the updated map at each iteration like we did using Array.reduce for the immutable version:

```
let totalLuggagePerPerson = (luggage: array<(string, int)>) => {
 open Belt
 let weights = MutableMap.String.make()
 Array.forEach(luggage, ((person, weight) as item) => {
   let curr = weights->MutableMap.String.
   getWithDefault(person, 0)
   weights->MutableMap.String.set(person, curr + weight)
 })
 weights
}
```

```
luggage->totalLuggagePerPerson(luggage)
 ->MutableMap.String.toArray
 ->Js.log
```

Console output:

```
[
 ["John", 342],
 ["Sarah", 87],
 ["Seth", 60]
]
```

Hash Set and Hash Map

HashSets and HashMaps are another way to represent mutable sets and maps in ReScript. The main advantage of using a HashSet/HashMap over other types of sets/maps is performance. Looking up a value in a Map or MutableMap will take longer as the number of mappings increases, while the time to look up a value in a HashMap stays roughly constant no matter how many mappings it contains.

In general, the API for HashSet/HashMap is very similar to the API MutableSet/MutableMap, but there are a few differences which I'll outline in the following.

Creating a Hash Set/Hash Map

Empty HashSets and HashMaps need to be provided with a "hint size" at creation time, through the ~hintSize named parameter. This can be seen as a rough estimate of how many elements the collection is expected to hold, although it's only an approximation so we don't need to worry about getting it exactly right:

```
let hashSet = Belt.HashSet.Int.make(~hintSize=50)
```

The hintSize is not required for HashSets and HashMaps initialized from arrays or lists:

```
let hashSet = Belt.HashSet.Int.fromArray([1, 1, 2, 3])
```

Accessing Hash Maps

Right now, HashMaps do not offer getWithDefault and getExn functions out of the box, only a get function that returns an optional value. However, we can pipe get into Belt.Option.getWithDefault or Belt.Option.getExn to get the same behaviors.

Hash Map Example

The differences between HashMap and MutableMap creation and access APIs are demonstrated in this version of the luggage example, implemented using a HashMap:

```
let totalLuggagePerPerson = (luggage: array<(string,
int)>) => {
 open Belt
 let weights = HashMap.String.make(~hintSize=10)
 Array.forEach(luggage, ((person, weight) as item) => {
   let curr = weights->HashMap.String.get(person)
     ->Option.getWithDefault(0)
   weights->HashMap.String.set(person, curr + weight)
 })
 weights
}
luggage->totalLuggagePerPerson->HashMap.String.toArray->Js.log
```

Console output:

```
[
 ["John", 342],
 ["Sarah", 87],
 ["Seth", 60]
]
```

Advanced Topic: Generic Hash Set/Hash Map Keys

If we are using a custom data type as the key to a HashSet or HashMap, we will have to define a custom hash function for that data type which takes in a value of that type and outputs some integer.

Just like how we made custom comparison modules using Belt. Id.MakeComparable, custom hashing modules are made using Belt. Id.MakeHashable. Here's a trivial example for integers (in practice, we would use Belt.HashSet.Int):

```
open Belt

module IntHash = Id.MakeHashable({
 type t = int
 let hash = x => x
 let eq = (a, b) => a == b
})

let hashset = HashSet.make(~hintSize=100, ~id=module(IntHash))

hashset->HashSet.add(1)
hashset->HashSet.add(1)
hashset->HashSet.add(1)
hashset->HashSet.add(2)

hashset->HashSet.size->Js.log
```

Console output:

2

Ideally, our hash function should be written such that two values that are not equal to each other (as defined by eq) will hash to different numbers. For example, if we wanted to make unique hashes for coordinates on a 10x10 grid in battleship, it might look like this:

```
module CoordHash = Belt.Id.MakeHashable({
  type t = (int, int)
  let hash = ((x, y)) => 100 * x + y
  let eq = (a, b) => a == b
})
```

The simple hash function defined earlier will give unique hashes as long as the values for each coordinate are between 0 and 99. For example, (0,0) will hash to 0, (9,9) will hash to 909, etc. This is more than adequate for our purposes, since all the coordinate values will be between 0 and 9.

More complex data types can require more complex hash functions, and it's not always possible to guarantee unique hashes. The important thing to remember is that your hash functions don't need to be perfect. If two different values hash to the same number (a **collision**), your hash table will still work, although a bad hash function that causes lots of collisions will degrade performance. If there are constraints on the possible keys, we can use that to simplify the hash function like we did in the previous example.

Beyond the differences involved in defining a comparable and a hashable, usage of generic HashSets and HashMaps is virtually the same as the other set/map APIs.

Here's the battleship Set example from earlier, reimplemented with a HashSet:

```
open Belt

module CoordHash = Id.MakeHashable({
 type t = (int, int)
 let hash = ((x, y)) => 100 * x + y
 let eq = (a, b) => a == b
})

let guessed = HashSet.fromArray([(1,1)], ~id=module(CoordHash))
let ships = HashSet.fromArray([(2,2), (2,3), (2,4)],
~id=module(CoordHash))

let checkCoord = ((x, y) as coord, guesses, ships) => {
 if HashSet.has(guesses, coord) {
   Js.log("already guessed")
 } else if HashSet.has(ships, coord) {
   Js.log("hit")
 } else {
   Js.log("miss")
 }
}

checkCoord((1, 1), guessed, ships)
checkCoord((0, 0), guessed, ships)
checkCoord((2, 2), guessed, ships)
```

Console output:

```
already guessed
miss
hit
```

Here's the battleship map example from earlier, reimplemented with a HashMap:

```
type grid = | Ship | Guessed

let board = Belt.HashMap.fromArray(
  [((2, 2), Ship), ((2, 3), Ship), ((2, 4), Ship), ((1, 1),
  Guessed)],
  ~id=module(CoordHash),
)

let checkCoord = ((x, y) as coord, board) => {
  switch Belt.HashMap.get(board, coord) {
    | Some(Guessed) => Js.log("already guessed")
    | Some(Ship) => Js.log("hit")
    | None => Js.log("miss")
  }
}

checkCoord((1, 1), board)
checkCoord((0, 0), board)
checkCoord((2, 2), board)
```

Dict

Dicts (dictionaries) are another way to represent key-value pairs in ReScript. Keys must be strings, and values can be any type as long as all the values are the same type.

Like records and objects, dicts are JavaScript objects at runtime. This means that we can safely pass dicts between ReScript code and JavaScript code, making them useful for interoperability. Unlike the other types of maps, we can directly log them with Js.log and serialize them into JSON.

Creating a Dict

Dicts can be created empty, or initialized from an array or list of key-value pairs:

```
let scores = Js.Dict.empty()
Js.log(scores)

let scores = Js.Dict.fromArray([("Player 1", 100), ("Player
2", 200)])
Js.log(scores)

let scores = Js.Dict.fromList(list{("Player 1", 100), ("Player
2", 200)})
Js.log(scores)
```

Console output:

```
{}
{"Player 1": 100, "Player 2": 200}
{"Player 1": 100, "Player 2": 200}
```

Accessing a Dict

The main access function for dicts is type-safe and returns an option, which can be pattern matched or handled with Belt.Option.getWithDefault or Belt.Option.getExn:

```
open Belt

let score1 = Js.Dict.get(scores, "Player 1")->Option.getExn

let score2 = Js.Dict.get(scores, "ashdgjasd")->Option.
getWithDefault(0)

Js.log2(score1, score2)
```

Console output:

```
100 0
```

Updating a Dict

As previously mentioned, dicts are mutable=:

```
let scores = Js.Dict.empty()
scores->Js.Dict.set("Player 1", 100)

Js.log(scores)
```

Console output:

```
{"Player 1": 100}
```

Serializing a Dict

Since dicts are just JavaScript objects at runtime, printing and serializing is simple.

We can print them directly using Js.log:

```
let scores = Js.Dict.fromArray([("Player 1", 100), ("Player
2", 200)])
Js.log(scores)
```

Console output:

```
{ "Player 1": 100, "Player 2": 200 }
```

Assuming the values of the dict also cleanly serialize to JSON, we can use a function like Js.Json.serializeExn to serialize the entire dict to a JSON string:

```
let scores = Js.Dict.fromArray([("Player 1", 100), ("Player
2", 200)])
let serialized = Js.Json.serializeExn(scores)
Js.log(serialized)
```

Console output:

```
'{ "Player 1": 100, "Player 2": 200 }'
```

If we need to serialize any of the other map types to JSON objects, we can convert them to a Dict. If the original map has something other than strings as keys, we'll need to convert the keys to strings.

Here's an example converting Belt.Map.String to Js.Dict:

```
open Belt
```

```
let scores = Map.String.fromArray([("Player 1", 100), ("Player
2", 200)])
let scoresDict = scores->Map.String.toArray->Js.Dict.fromArray
```

```
Js.log(scoresDict)
```

Console output:

```
{ "Player 1": 100, "Player 2": 200 }
```

Dicts can also be used to model the shape of objects parsed from JSON, when the number and names of an object's properties are not predetermined. When the property names are known beforehand, records or objects should be used instead.

In the final chapter, we'll revisit dicts again when we discuss strategies for parsing and validating JSON payloads.

Which Collection Should I Use?

In this chapter, we covered three different types of sets and four different types of maps available in ReScript's standard library. For newcomers to the language, it can be confusing to determine which one to use. For many use cases, which collection you choose is entirely up to your own preference, but there are some cases when a specific type of set/map is better than the others.

Let's start with sets first. The three different types of sets that we covered are Set, MutableSet, and HashSet. Refer to the table at the beginning of the chapter to see a side-by-side comparison.

HashSets should be used for collections that are expected to be very large since they are more performant, while regular Sets offer immutability and ordered keys in exchange for slightly worse performance.

Since Set and MutableSet are implemented as binary trees under the hood, they are actually quite performant, although still not as good as HashSets. Set and MutableSet lookups take logarithmic time based on the size of the set, while HashSets with well-designed hash functions have constant-time lookup regardless of the size of the collection. The caveat here is "well-designed": if you have a generic HashSet with a bad hash function that leads to tons of collisions, then the performance may be worse than a regular Set!

Here's a checklist to help determine which type of set to use:

> Use `Belt.Set` if we want immutability or ordering with reasonable performance.
>
> Use `Belt.HashSet` if we want the best possible performance, we don't care about the sort order of the values in the set, and the set will contain integers, strings, or a data type that we can write a good hash function for.
>
> If none of the above, use either `Belt.Set` or `Belt.MutableSet`.

171

Next, we'll discuss maps. The four different types of maps that we covered are Map, MutableMap, HashMap, and Dict. Refer to the table at the beginning of the chapter for a side-by-side comparison.

Dict should be used in situations when we want to easily deserialize or serialize the mapping to JSON or when we need to pass mappings between JavaScript and ReScript. The performance characteristics of Map/MutableMap/HashMap are similar to the performance comparisons I made for Set/MutableSet/HashSet, and as such the guidance for which type of map to use is similar to the guidance for sets.

Here's a checklist to help determine which type of map to use:

> Use `Belt.Map` if we need immutability or ordered keys.

> Use `Js.Dict` if we need to serialize the data to JSON, we want to pass the data to JavaScript, or the keys are strings.

> Use `Belt.HashMap` if we want the best possible performance, we don't care about the sort order of the keys in the map, and the keys are integers, strings, or a data type that we can write a good hash function for.

> If none of the above, use `Belt.Map` or `Belt.MutableMap`.

CHAPTER 7

Modules

Modules are groupings of functions and type definitions that allow us to organize and reuse code in complex programs. Every file in ReScript is its own module, but we can also define our own modules inside of files.

Modules and module signatures are very important for writing software in ReScript, because they serve several key purposes:

Namespacing – Modules allow the programmer to differentiate between functions/bindings with the same name declared in different places (e.g., `Belt.Array.map`, `Js.Array2.map`, `Js.Array.map`). This allows the programmer to use and write libraries without worrying about collisions between common function names.

Abstraction – Module signatures allow the programmer to expose a particular API without revealing its underlying details. For example, we could hide the internal types and helper functions a data structure uses. In a typical object-oriented language, this could be accomplished by using interfaces and private methods; in ReScript this role is fulfilled by module signatures.

© Danny Yang 2023
D. Yang, *Introducing ReScript*, https://doi.org/10.1007/978-1-4842-8888-7_7

Code reuse – Something defined in one module can be reused in other modules to reduce code duplication. In object-oriented languages, one would typically go about this via inheritance or composition. Composition is still possible in ReScript, and we also have access to **functors**, which are like functions that operate on modules instead of values.

Files as Modules

Every ReScript file is implicitly a module, and the module's name is the capitalized form of the file's name. The file Hello.res will correspond to a module named Hello.

Module names are always capitalized, so it's a good idea to capitalize ReScript files' names to match their module names. For example, use Hello.res instead of hello.res, since the module name will always be Hello.

All files are treated as modules in the same scope, and folders are ignored. This means that no two .res files in a ReScript project can share the same name each other, even if they are in different directories.

Defining Modules

Modules can also be defined inside of files. Module definitions look similar to let bindings, except they use the module keyword. Module names must be capitalized, and the contents of the module are wrapped in curly braces:

```
module MyModule = {
 type myType = int
 let hello = () => Js.log("hello")
}
```

Anything that we would put in a file can go into a module definition: this includes type definitions, let bindings, function definitions, and other module definitions.

Nested modules are a common pattern for organizing complex APIs – this can be seen in the standard library. For example, the function `Belt.Array.get` is inside the `Array` module, which is inside the `Belt` module. Conceptually, it can be modeled as such:

```
module Belt = {
  module Array = {
    let get = ...
  }
}
```

Module definitions can have the same name as long as they are in different scopes (see `Belt.Array` and `Js.Array`). However, just like how file names need to be unique, modules in the same scope have to have unique names. The following is not allowed:

```
module MyModule = {}
```

```
module MyModule = {}
```

Compiler output:

```
Multiple definition of the module name MyModule.
Names must be unique in a given structure or signature.
```

Using Modules

We can reference the functions and values defined inside a module by using the same notation as accessing fields from records:

```
module MyModule = {
 type myType = int
 let myValue = 1
 let hello = () => Js.log("hello")
}
```

```
let x = MyModule.myValue
MyModule.hello()
```

Console output:

```
hello
```

The types from a module can be referenced and used as part of signatures and new type definitions:

```
type newType1 = MyModule.myType
type newType2 = array<MyModule.myType>
```

```
let y : MyModule.myType = 1
```

This is also how we would reference the contents of other files. For example, say we had a file called Hello.res with the following contents:

```
let helloWorld = () => Js.log("hello, world")
```

We can use it in another file Myfile.res:

```
Hello.helloWorld()
```

Compiling the project and running Myfile.bs.js prints the following in console:

```
hello, world
```

When accessing something inside a nested module, we have to list each enclosing module, as we've already seen with examples involving the standard library:

```
module MyModule = {
 module MyNestedModule = {
   let x = "blah"
 }
}
MyModule.MyNestedModule.x->Js.log
```

Console output:

```
blah
```

Opening Modules

Having to type out the fully qualified names of every function we use can be tiresome, especially if we're working with a lot of nested modules.

As seen in previous chapters, we can open a module to make its contents visible in the current scope. This lets us avoid having to write the module's name when accessing its contents. We can see this in action using the previous nested module example:

```
module MyModule = {
 module MyNestedModule = {
   let x = "blah"
 }
}
```

```
MyModule.MyNestedModule.x->Js.log
```

```
open MyModule
MyNestedModule.x->Js.log
```

```
open MyModule.MyNestedModule
x->Js.log
```

Console output:

```
blah
blah
blah
```

Opening a module is not the same as importing a declaration in another language. All modules not hidden by a signature are visible from other modules, so you're not required to import anything. Opening a module only makes the module's contents easier to access by making their names shorter. Additionally, while other languages may only allow imports at the top level or at the beginning of each file, ReScript allows us to open modules in any scope.

Be careful to avoid unintentional shadowing when opening modules – opening a module will cause the module's bindings to shadow any bindings inside the current scope. Usually, this mistake is not a big deal – if the shadowed binding is a different type, then the code will not compile. However, if the shadowed binding is the same type then this may go unnoticed.

In the following code snippet, opening `MyModule.MyNestedModule` causes its binding for x to shadow the binding we declared earlier, resulting in an unexpected value being printed:

```
let x = 1

open MyModule.MyNestedModule
x->Js.log
```

Console output:

```
blah
```

Thankfully, the compiler emits a warning when opening a module shadows an existing binding. Using open! instead of open will silence the warning, but be careful and deliberate in its usage.

```
This open statement shadows the value identifier x (which is
later used).
```

178

Shadowing in the Standard Library

There is one common case where unintended shadowing can trip up newcomers. As described in an earlier chapter, opening the Belt standard library changes the behavior of array indexing. Therefore, files that have open Belt at the top and files that do not will have different behaviors when indexing arrays.

In the first example, everything works fine. We don't open any modules and we fully qualify Belt.Array:

```
let double = arr => {
 arr->Belt.Array.map(x => x * 2)
}

let triple = arr => {
 arr->Belt.Array.map(x => x * 3)
}

let myArr = [1, 2, 3]->double->triple
Js.log(myArr[0] === 6)
```

Console output:

```
true
```

Opening Belt at the top of the file makes things more concise, allowing us to write Array.map instead of Belt.Array.map. Unfortunately, the behavior and type signature of array indexing have changed due to shadowing, and our code no longer compiles:

```
open Belt

let double = arr => {
 arr->Array.map(x => x * 2)
}
```

```
let triple = arr => {
 arr->Array.map(x => x * 3)
}
```

```
let myArr = [1, 2, 3]->double->triple
Js.log(myArr[0] === 6)
```

Compiler output:

```
This has type: int
Somewhere wanted: option<int>
```

If we open Belt.Array only in the functions where we need it, we can eliminate the clunky prefixes without any risk of shadowing or unintended behavior:

```
let double = arr => {
 open Belt.Array
 arr->map(x => x * 2)
}
```

```
let triple = arr => {
 open Belt.Array
 arr->map(x => x * 3)
}
```

```
let myArr = [1, 2, 3]->double->triple
Js.log(myArr[0] === 6)
```

Console output:

```
true
```

Although the last example is a bit contrived since each function only uses Belt.Array.map once, I hope you see my point. We don't have to open every module we might use at the top of the file – opening modules in a nested scope can help avoid unintentional shadowing.

Destructuring a Module

If we only want to access a few functions/bindings in a module, one alternative to opening a module is destructuring. Destructuring a module is similar to destructuring a record, allowing us to easily access only the contents we care about while minimizing the risk of accidental shadowing.

The syntax is the same as destructuring a record:

```
module MyModule = {
 type myType = int
 let myValue = 1
 let hello = () => Js.log("hello")
}

let {myValue, hello} = module(MyModule)

Js.log(myValue)
hello()
```

Console output:

```
1
hello
```

To avoid shadowing existing bindings, we can also assign aliases to the destructured names:

```
let myValue = 0
let {myValue : newName} = module(MyModule)

Js.log2(myValue, newName)
```

Console output:

```
0 1
```

Module Examples

Now that we've covered the rules of writing and using modules, let's go over some practical examples by implementing some modules for immutable data structures.

I won't go over these implementations line-by-line, the purpose of these examples is just to show how concepts from previous chapters can be used together with modules.

Our first example is a module that implements an efficient immutable stack using a List. It defines a set of simple stack operations: creating a new stack, push, pop, peek, and getting the size of the stack. As with other immutable data structures, operations do not mutate the input stack – they simply return a new stack with the operation applied.

Notice that the size function is actually just an alias for Belt.List.size, and the get function provides null safety by returning an option:

```
module ListStack = {
  // initializing a new empty stack
  let new = () => list{}

  // return new stack with additional element
  let push = (stack, element) => {
    list{element, ...stack}
  }

  // return top element of the stack as an option
  let peek = stack => {
    switch stack {
    | list{hd, ..._} => Some(hd)
    | _ => None
    }
  }
```

```
// return new stack without top element
let pop = stack => {
  switch stack {
  | list{_, ...tl} => tl
  | _ => stack
  }
}

// return number of elements in the stack
let size = Belt.List.size
}
```

The module can be used as such:

```
let stack = ListStack.new()
let stack' = stack->ListStack.push(10)
   ->ListStack.push(100)
   ->ListStack.push(1000)
   ->ListStack.pop

stack'->ListStack.size->Js.log
stack'->ListStack.peek->Belt.Option.getExn->Js.log
```

Console output:

```
2
100
```

One important distinction between modules and classes: our module is not a class that contains a list; it is a collection of functions that operates on a list. There is no "instance" of ListStack or anything wrapping the list, the stack is just the list itself, and ListStack is a namespace containing functions that manipulate lists as if they were stacks.

Next, we have an immutable map implemented using a List. In this module, the underlying data type is a list of key-value pairs. To contrast with the safe peek function of the stack, here we make the get function throw if the mapping is not found:

```
module ListMap = {
 open Belt

 let new = () => list{}

 // return a new map with mapping for k removed
 let remove = (map, k) => {
   List.keep(map, ((key, _)) => key !== k)
 }

 // return a new map with added mapping for k -> v
 let set = (map, k, v) => {
   list{(k, v), ...remove(map, k)}
 }

 // return mapped value for k, or throws
 let rec get = (map, k) => {
   switch map {
   | list{} => raise(Not_found)
   | list{(key, val), ..._} if key === k => val
   | list{_, ...rest} => get(rest, k)
   }
 }

 let size = List.size
}
```

Here's how the ListMap module can be used:

```
let map = ListMap.new()
let map' = map->ListMap.set("duck", 10)
  ->ListMap.set("chicken", 25)
let map'' = map'->ListMap.remove("duck")

map->ListMap.size->Js.log
map'->ListMap.size->Js.log
map''->ListMap.size->Js.log
map'->ListMap.get("duck")->Js.log
```

Console output:

```
0
2
1
10
```

This is a pretty inefficient implementation of a map because we have to go through the entire list whenever we look up or modify a mapping. Remember that we're only using this as an example here – for real use cases, Belt.Map is much better.

A final example: an immutable priority queue. This data structure is implemented using a binary tree, and is also a good demonstration of variants and pattern matching. By taking advantage of recursion to traverse the tree, each function only needs a single switch that handles just the current node (the children are handled by recursive calls):

```
module PriorityQueue = {
  type priority = int
  type rec queue<'a> = Empty | Node(priority, 'a, queue<'a>,
  queue<'a>)
```

```
let empty = Empty

// return new queue w/ added element
let rec insert = (queue, prio, elt) => {
  switch queue {
  | Empty => Node(prio, elt, Empty, Empty)
  | Node(p, e, left, right) =>
    if prio <= p {
      Node(prio, elt, insert(right, p, e), left)
    } else {
      Node(p, e, insert(right, prio, elt), left)
    }
  }
}

// return new queue w/o lowest priority element,
// which is always the topmost node
let rec pop = queue => {
  switch queue {
  | Empty => queue
  | Node(_, _, left, Empty) => left
  | Node(_, _, Empty, right) => right
  | Node(_, _, Node(lprio, lelt, _, _) as left, Node(rprio,
    relt, _, _) as right) =>
    if lprio <= rprio {
      Node(lprio, lelt, pop(left), right)
    } else {
      Node(rprio, relt, left, pop(right))
    }
  }
}
```

```
// return the lowest-priority element in the queue as an
// optional tuple of (priority, element)
let peek = queue => {
  switch queue {
  | Empty => None
  | Node(prio, elt, _, _) as queue => Some((prio, elt))
  }
}

// return size of the queue
let rec size = queue => {
  switch queue {
  | Empty => 0
  | Node(_, _, left, right) => 1 + size(left) + size(right)
  }
}
}
```

Here's how it would be used:

```
let pq = PriorityQueue.empty
->PriorityQueue.insert(5, "task A")
->PriorityQueue.insert(10, "task B")
->PriorityQueue.insert(1, "task C")

let first = pq->PriorityQueue.peek

let pq' = pq->PriorityQueue.pop
let second = pq'->PriorityQueue.peek

let pq'' = pq'->PriorityQueue.pop
let third = pq''->PriorityQueue.peek
```

```
switch (first, second, third) {
| (Some((p1, j1)), Some((p2, j2)), Some((p3, j3))) => {
   Js.log2(p1, j1)
   Js.log2(p2, j2)
   Js.log2(p3, j3)
 }
| _ => Js.log("something went wrong")
}
```

Console output:

```
1 task C
5 task A
10 task B
```

As with other immutable data structures, updating this priority queue doesn't change any state, and we don't lose any information about the past. After we've popped items off to create pq'', we can access pq and pq' to see the previous states.

Module Signatures

Module signatures are like a type signature for modules. They serve the purpose of separating the interface of a module from its implementation. Multiple modules can implement the same signature, allowing better abstraction and code reuse via functors. Additionally, signatures can be used to restrict which values in a module are visible to its users, which helps programmers avoid leaking implementation details outside the module.

Interface Files

For file-level modules, signatures are defined via an interface file with the same name and a different extension (`.resi`).

For example, say we have a file named `MyModule.res` with the following contents:

```
let secret = 1
let public = secret * 2
```

Without an interface, `MyModule.secret` and `MyModule.public` can be accessed outside of the file. Say we want to hide the existence of `secret` outside the module. To do this, we can define an interface for `MyModule` inside a `MyModule.resi` which only contains the signature for x:

```
let public: int
```

Now, `MyModule.public` is still visible outside the module, but `MyModule.secret` is not.

Defining Module Signatures

Just like modules, module signatures can also be defined inside of files. The definition looks very similar to a module definition, except using `module type` instead of `module`. Names of module signatures must be capitalized.

Unlike interface files, inline module signatures aren't automatically matched up with a module implementation. Instead, each module implementation can choose which signature it implements.

Here's what the previous example would look like if `MyModule` was defined inside a file:

```
module type MySig = {
 let public: int
}
```

```
module MyModule : MySig = {
 let secret = 1
 let public = secret * 2
}
```

Let's go over a more complex example to show how multiple modules can implement the same signature.

Here's a signature that represents an immutable stack. Since we don't know the underlying data type representing the stack, we specify that any modules implementing the signature must define a type t<'a> to represent a stack containing elements of some generic type 'a. This allows us to define the signature of the other functions in the module based on that type:

```
module type ImmStack = {
 type t<'a>
 let new: unit => t<'a>
 let push: (t<'a>, 'a) => t<'a>
 let peek: t<'a> => option<'a>
 let pop: t<'a> => t<'a>
 let size: t<'a> => int
}
```

Looking back at our ListStack implementation from earlier, I mentioned that the module contains a collection of functions that operates on lists. This means that functions from that module can be applied to any list. In other words, the implementation details are leaked. For example, the following snippet would be allowed:

```
let stack = ListStack.new()
->ListStack.push(1)
->ListStack.push(2)
->Belt.List.reverse

let top = stack->ListStack.peek
```

Leaking implementation details is undesirable, because it allows users to perform operations that violate the invariants of our module. It doesn't make sense for functions like Belt.List.reverse to be applied to our stacks, since it breaks the definition of a stack.

In order to prevent illegal operations on our stacks, we can hide the underlying data type for the ListStack module using a signature. If the code outside the module does not know that ListStack is backed by a list, then they can't use regular list operations to illegally manipulate the stack.

To do this, we just need to add a definition for the underlying data type t<'a> and make our ListStack module implement the ImmStack signature:

```
module ListStack : ImmStack = {

 type t<'a> = list<'a>

 // Rest of ListStack implementation follows
 ...
}
```

Although ListStack still manipulates lists under the hood, that detail is no longer revealed to users of the module. From the perspective of other modules, all ListStack functions operate on values of type ListStack.t, and the only way to create a ListStack.t is with ListStack.new. Trying to call standard library list functions on ListStack.t values outside the module will give a type error, showing that we have successfully hidden its implementation details:

```
This has type: ListStack.t<'a>
Somewhere wanted: Belt.List.t<'b> (defined as list<'b>)
```

Now, let's define another module that can match the ImmStack signature. The implementer of the module can define t<'a> as anything they want, so stacks backed by other data structures are also valid implementations of ImmStack. This time, we'll define a stack module that stores data using an array.

Since arrays don't support immutable updates, this is actually a horribly inefficient implementation because it copies the whole array every time we push or pop a value. Luckily for us the user of the module doesn't have to know that, its signature means that it can be used exactly the same as ListStack:

```
module ArrayStack: ImmStack = {
  type t<'a> = array<'a>

  let new = () => []
  let push = (stack, element) => {
    let copy = stack->Js.Array2.copy
    copy->Js.Array2.push(element)->ignore
    copy
  }

  let peek = stack => {
    if Js.Array2.length(stack) === 0 {
      None
    } else {
      Some(stack[Js.Array2.length(stack) - 1])
    }
  }
}
```

```
let pop = stack => {
  let copy = stack->Js.Array2.copy
  copy->Js.Array2.pop->ignore
  copy
}

let size = Js.Array2.length
}
```

We can also define a third stack implementation using a custom variant type. The discerning reader will notice that this is essentially the same as a list-based stack, with Empty being analogous to list{} and Item(a, b) being analogous to list{a, ...b}. Therefore, this is significantly more efficient than the array-based stack:

```
module MyStack: ImmStack = {
 type rec t<'a> = Empty | Item('a, t<'a>)

 let new = () => Empty

 let push = (stack, element) => {
   Item(element, stack)
 }

 let peek = stack => {
   switch stack {
   | Item(top, _) => Some(top)
   | _ => None
   }
 }
}
```

```
let pop = stack => {
  switch stack {
  | Item(_, rest) => rest
  | _ => stack
  }
}

let rec size = stack => {
  switch stack {
  | Item(_, rest) => 1 + size(rest)
  | _ => 0
  }
 }
}
```

Having multiple modules matching the same signature is nice when we need to substitute one module for another, but that's not all. By combining what modules and signatures with functors, we can finally unlock the true power and reusability of modules.

Functors

Functors are essentially functions for modules: they take in some modules as input, and output a new module. This allows us to create new modules by combining and extending existing modules.

Functors become extremely powerful when combined with the abstraction of module signatures. Just like how functions are defined to accept values that match a particular type, functors are defined so that they accept any module that matches a particular signature. This allows the same functor to be reused on many different input modules, just like how the same function can be called with many different possible arguments.

Defining and Using Functors

To demonstrate how to write and use functors, let's define a functor that takes in an immutable stack module and returns a mutable stack module.

Functor definitions look like a combination of module definition and function definitions. Our functor MakeMutableStack accepts a module that implements ImmStack and uses its functions in another module definition. The name of the input can be anything, as long as it is capitalized, and it will be referred to by that name inside the module definition:

```
module MakeMutableStack = (Stack: ImmStack) => {
  let new = () => ref(Stack.new())

  let push = (stack, element) => {
    stack := stack.contents->Stack.push(element)
  }

  let peek = stack => {
    Stack.peek(stack.contents)
  }

  let pop = stack => {
    stack := Stack.pop(stack.contents)
  }

  let size = stack => Stack.size(stack.contents)
}
```

This functor is pretty simple – it just stores the immutable stack in a reference and mutates the reference with the updated stack after each update.

Using the functor to define a new module is just like calling a function. We can reuse the same functor to all of our modules that implement ImmStack to create three new modules for mutable stacks – neat!

```
module MyMutableStack = MakeMutableStack(MyStack)

module MutableArrayStack = MakeMutableStack(ArrayStack)

module MutableListStack = MakeMutableStack(ListStack)
```

Inputs to functors are required to be annotated with signatures, but we may also optionally provide a signature for the output of a functor. Let's define a signature for mutable stacks called MutStack, and use it to describe our functor:

```
module type MutStack = {
  type t<'a>
  let new: unit => t<'a>
  let push: (t<'a>, 'a) => unit
  let peek: t<'a> => option<'a>
  let pop: t<'a> => unit
  let size: t<'a> => int
}

module MakeMutableStack = (Stack: ImmStack): MutStack => {
  type t<'a> = ref<Stack.t<'a>>

  // rest of MakeMutableStack follows
}
```

Now, every module defined using MakeMutableStack will implement MutStack. The type signature of the entire functor is ImmStack => MutStack.

Extending Modules

Functors can be used to extend existing modules with new functionality. For example, let's say that we want a way to extend any ImmStack module with fromArray and toArray functions. Regardless of the backing data type for the stack, having these functions will help us debug our code and make interoperating with JavaScript easier.

Instead of writing fromArray and toArray separately for each ImmStack implementation, we can just implement them once in a functor and reuse that for all ImmStack modules.

First, let's extend our signature for ImmStack with our new operations by defining a new signature. To avoid redeclaring all the ImmStack functions, we'll use the include keyword which does this copy-pasting for us:

```
module type ExtendedImmStack = {
  include ImmStack

  let fromArray: array<'a> => t<'a>
  let toArray: t<'a> => array<'a>
}
```

Next, we'll write a functor that takes an ImmStack and creates an ExtendedImmStack. We'll use include to copy the implementation for the module we pass in, and define the two new functions. For these two functions, we'll use the invariant that the top of the stack corresponds to the last element in the array:

```
module ExtendImmStack : ImmStack => ExtendedImmStack = (Stack:
ImmStack) => {
  include Stack

  let fromArray = (arr: array<'a>) => {
    Js.Array2.reduce(arr, (stack, el) => Stack.push(stack,
    el), Stack.new())
  }
```

```
let toArray = (stack: Stack.t<'a>) => {
    let arr = []
    let current = ref(stack)
    while Stack.size(current.contents) > 0 {
        // we make sure the stack is non-empty in the loop
        guard, so getExn is safe
        let next_val = Stack.peek(current.contents)->Belt.
        Option.getExn
        arr->Js.Array2.push(next_val)->ignore
        current := Stack.pop(current.contents)
    }
    Js.Array2.reverseInPlace(arr)
    }
}
```

We can apply this functor to add these operations to all our `ImmStack` implementations:

```
module MyExtendedStack = ExtendImmStack(MyStack)

module ExtendedArrayStack = ExtendImmStack(ArrayStack)

module ExtendedListStack = ExtendImmStack(ListStack)
```

With this extension, our stack modules are much easier to print and debug. Without converting to an array, printing the stack would have looked something like this:

```
let s = MyExtendedStack.fromArray([1, 2, 3])
let s' = s->MyExtendedStack.push(4)

s'->Js.log
```

Console output (terrible):

```
{ _0: 4, _1: { _0: 3, _1: { _0: 2, _1: [Object] } } }
```

By using our new function to convert our stack to an array before printing, it's much more readable:

```
let s = MyExtendedStack.fromArray([1, 2, 3])
let s' = s->MyExtendedStack.push(4)

s'->MyExtendedStack.toArray->Js.log
```

Console output (nice!):

```
[1, 2, 3, 4]
```

Although our functor's implementations of fromArray and toArray aren't the most efficient possible implementations for ArrayStack (which is already an array under the hood), there are benefits to having a single implementation. There is less code to maintain, and we don't have to make sure that each separate implementation respects the same invariants.

Functors in the Standard Library

Functors are an important part of ReScript's standard library, because standard library functions and modules need to be able to handle all kinds of data types.

We've already used functors in an earlier chapter – both Belt. Id.MakeComparable and Belt.Id.MakeHashable are examples of functors. They allow the sets and maps provided in the standard library to be used with any data type we want, as long as we provide a module that defines comparison or hashing operations for that data type.

For example, the signature of Belt.Id.MakeComparable looks like this:

```
module MakeComparable: (M: {
 type t
 let cmp: (t, t) => int
}) => Comparable with type t = M.t
```

It's a functor that takes in any module that defines a type t and a cmp function for comparing two values of that type, and outputs a module that matches the Comparable signature.

Recall how we used this functor to create a new module to compare pairs of integers in our battleship example:

```
module CoordCmp = Belt.Id.MakeComparable({
  type t = (int, int)
  let cmp = (a, b) => Pervasives.compare(a, b)
})
```

One interesting thing to note in the previous snippets is the use of anonymous modules and module signatures. We do not have to declare a module or signature beforehand to use it in a functor; we can provide the definition or signature in-line.

If we were to modify the previous snippet to use a named module, it would look something like this:

```
module Coord = {
  type t = (int, int)
  let cmp = (a, b) => Pervasives.compare(a, b)
}

module CoordCmp = Belt.Id.MakeComparable(Coord)
```

Final Thoughts

In this chapter, we discussed how to define and use modules in ReScript, and how to transform modules using functors. Modules are especially vital to writing large software applications in ReScript, because they enable namespacing, abstraction, and code reuse.

Organizing code into modules allows us to group different parts of the application logically, so that it's not just a collection of functions and types at the top level. Modules and signatures also allow us to define interfaces between different parts of our application and hide unnecessary implementation details. Finally, functors allow us to operate on a higher level of abstraction, allowing us to transform modules and reuse or extend their functionality.

With this chapter, we've covered all of the main language features in ReScript as well as many fundamental concepts in functional programming. You should be well-equipped to write clean, organized, and efficient programs in ReScript. In the final chapter, we'll apply these concepts to the real world: we'll discuss how to write ReScript programs that interoperate with JavaScript, and integrate JavaScript libraries into a simple ReScript web application.

CHAPTER 8

JavaScript Interoperability

Interoperability with JavaScript is one of the highlights of ReScript that makes it well-suited for web development. It allows ReScript programs to use the huge ecosystem of JavaScript libraries that many web developers are already familiar with. Interoperability also makes it easy to convert parts of an existing JavaScript code base into ReScript while maintaining compatibility with existing code, whether for experimentation purposes or as part of a wider migration effort.

In this chapter, we'll discuss the runtime representations of various ReScript data types, how to import and use JavaScript values or functions from ReScript and vice versa, and strategies for parsing and validating JSON. Finally, we'll see those techniques in action by writing a simple web application entirely using ReScript.

Calling JavaScript from ReScript

Since JavaScript functions don't come with types, it's up to the programmer to define their signatures when they are called from ReScript. Signatures for external functions are called "bindings," and they basically tell the ReScript compiler, "there's no definition in ReScript for it, but a function exists somewhere with this signature."

© Danny Yang 2023
D. Yang, *Introducing ReScript*, https://doi.org/10.1007/978-1-4842-8888-7_8

Let's go over a simple example of importing a JavaScript module and writing ReScript bindings.

First, we'll create a simple JavaScript file called jsmodule.js that contains a single function that we'll be calling from ReScript:

```
let getCurrentYear = () => {
    return new Date().getFullYear();
}

exports.getCurrentYear = getCurrentYear
```

Next, we'll create a Rescript file called CallJsDemo.res. Inside, we'll write the binding for the function. Bindings for both values and functions are structured according to the following format:

```
<annotation>
external <ReScript binding name>: <type signature> =
"<JavaScript name>"
```

In our case, the binding will look like this:

```
@module("./jsmodule")
external getCurrentYear: () => int = "getCurrentYear"
```

Let's break down the components of the binding:

> @module("./jsmodule") – This tells the compiler which module we are importing the function from.
>
> getCurrentYear – This is the name that we'll use to call the function from ReScript. It doesn't have to match the name of the function in JavaScript!
>
> () => int – This is the type signature of the function, which takes in no arguments and returns an integer.

"getCurrentYear" – This is the real name of the JavaScript function we're binding to.

Now that we have a binding, we can call the function just like we would call any other ReScript function:

```
@module("./jsmodule")
external getCurrentYear: () => int = "getCurrentYear"

getCurrentYear()->Js.log
```

When the @module annotation is used, ReScript knows to automatically import the module at the top of the compiled output, which looks like this:

```
'use strict';

var JsModule = require("./jsmodule");

function getCurrentYear(prim) {
 return JsModule.getCurrentYear();
}

console.log(JsModule.getCurrentYear());

exports.getCurrentYear = getCurrentYear;
```

When we run the compiled code, we can see that it successfully calls the JavaScript function and prints the output. Note that the output may be different depending on what year you are reading this!

```
> node src/CallJsDemo.bs.js
2022
```

Sometimes, automatically importing a module is not desirable, particularly when binding to the standard library. For example, let's say we want to call JSON.parse. If we use @module("JSON"), the compiler will try to import a module called JSON at the beginning of the file. To avoid this, we can use @scoped instead:

```
@scope("JSON") @val
external parse: string => 'a = "parse"

let obj = parse("{}")
```

The compiled output contains no imports:

```
var obj = JSON.parse("{}");
```

There are other annotations that are useful for binding to JavaScript, which we'll go over in later examples:

> @val for global values not in any scope
>
> @variadic for variadic functions (functions that take a variable number of arguments)
>
> @get and @set for object properties
>
> @send for methods

It's also worth mentioning that functions are not the only thing that we can write bindings for. For example, if we want to share constants between JavaScript and ReScript, we can. As long as there's a way to express the value's type in ReScript, we can write a binding for it.

We'll go over examples of different types of annotations and bindings later in the chapter.

Embedding Raw JavaScript in ReScript Files

In addition to writing bindings to call external JavaScript functions, we can also embed raw JavaScript directly inside ReScript files. This is not recommended for production code because it's not type-safe, but it can be useful for practicing or if we want to quickly prototype something.

To embed top-level JavaScript definitions and code, use %%raw() with the JavaScript code snippet surrounded by backticks:

```
%%raw(`
 // put your Javascript code here!
`)
```

To actually call functions defined in those blocks, we need to bind them just like we would any other external JavaScript code:

```
%%raw(`
function hello() {
   console.log("hello!");
}
`)

@val external hello: () => unit = "hello"

hello()
```

Console output:

```
hello!
```

If we want to embed an expression instead of an entire code block, we can use %raw() (note the single %):

```
let hello = %raw(`
 function() {
   console.log("hello!");
 }
`) hello()
```

Console output:

```
hello!
```

Calling ReScript from JavaScript

Now, let's show how ReScript can be called from JavaScript. Since ReScript files are compiled into JavaScript files, calling ReScript from JavaScript is more or less the same as calling any other JavaScript file.

Exporting Values from ReScript

By default, all top-level values declared in a ReScript file are exported when they're compiled into a JavaScript module.

The ReScript file here:

```
let a = [1, 2, 3]
let b = a[0]
```

Compiles to this JavaScript:

```
'use strict';

var Caml_array = require("rescript/lib/js/caml_array.js");

var a = [1, 2, 3];

var b = Caml_array.get(a, 0);

exports.a = a;
exports.b = b;
```

To limit which values are exported, we can create an interface file (.resi). For files that have an associated interface, only the values declared in the interface are exported from the module.

We can add a .resi file with the following contents to avoid exporting a from the previous example:

```
let b : int
```

The output JavaScript code does not export that value anymore:

```
'use strict';

var Caml_array = require("rescript/lib/js/caml_array.js");

var a = [1, 2, 3];

var b = Caml_array.get(a, 0);

exports.b = b;
```

Using ReScript Modules from JavaScript

Let's go over an example of how we would actually use a ReScript module from JavaScript.

The ReScript module we're using will look familiar: it is the ListStack module from the previous chapter. Make a file called ListStack.res with the following contents:

```
type t<'a> = list<'a>

let new = () => list{}

let push = (stack, element) => {
  list{element, ...stack}
}

let peek = stack => {
  switch stack {
  | list{hd, ..._} => Some(hd)
  | _ => None
  }
}
```

```
let pop = stack => {
 switch stack {
 | list{_, ...tl} => tl
 | _ => stack
 }
}
```

```
let size = Belt.List.size
```

Then, in the same directory, make a JavaScript file called usestack.js with the following contents:

```
var ListStack = require("./ListStack.bs");
```

```
var stack = ListStack.$$new();
```

```
var values = [9, 3, 5]
```

```
values.forEach(x => {
    stack = ListStack.push(stack, x);
});
```

```
while (ListStack.size(stack) !== 0) {
    console.log(ListStack.peek(stack))
    stack = ListStack.pop(stack)
}
```

Notice that the ReScript module is imported and used just like any other JS module. The only difference is that the new function had to be escaped since "new" is a keyword in JavaScript.

To run the example, first compile the ReScript file to JS and then use node to run usestack.js. The terminal will show the following:

```
5
3
9
```

Shared Data Types

Many data types in ReScript compile directly to logical JavaScript equivalents, so they can be passed back and forth between ReScript and JavaScript without issues. The following is a chart mapping ReScript data types to their JavaScript runtime representations:

- string -> string

- bool -> boolean

- float -> number

- object/record/Dict -> object

- array/tuple -> array

- unit -> undefined

- module -> module

In some cases, multiple ReScript data types can map to the same JavaScript data type; for example, both arrays and tuples in ReScript compile to JavaScript arrays.

To demonstrate why this matters, we'll use some JavaScript functions that operate on arrays with two elements:

```
let makePair = (x, y) => [x, y];
let getX = pair => pair[0];
let getY = pair => pair[1];
```

In ReScript, since both tuples and arrays compile to JavaScript arrays, either type can be used for these functions. This gives us the ability to choose the representation that is most compatible with our use case.

This is what the bindings for these functions would look like if we chose to use arrays:

```
%%raw(`
let makePair = (x, y) => [x, y];
let getX = pair => pair[0];
let getY = pair => pair[1];
`)
```

```
@val external makePairArray: (int, int) => array<int> =
"makePair"
@val external getXArray: array<int> => int = "getX"
@val external getYArray: array<int> => int = "getY"

let pair = makePairArray(3, 5)
getXArray(pair)->Js.log
getYArray(pair)->Js.log
```

And here's how we would write bindings for these functions using tuples:

```
@val external makePairTuple: (int, int) => (int, int) =
"makePair"
@val external getXTuple: ((int, int)) => int = "getX"
@val external getYTuple: ((int, int)) => int = "getY"

let pair = makePairTuple(3, 5)
getXTuple(pair)->Js.log
getYTuple(pair)->Js.log
```

By using different names, we can create separate bindings with different types which bind to the same function. Both sets of bindings can exist at the same time in our ReScript program, and ReScript treats them as different functions even though they are the same JavaScript function under the hood.

Declaring multiple bindings with specialized types for the same JavaScript function is a common pattern – JavaScript libraries are generally less strict about what types are allowed, and having more specialized type signatures allows ReScript's typechecker to provide more guarantees that we're using these functions correctly.

Other data types can also be shared between ReScript and JavaScript, but require special considerations.

Integers

Like floats, integers also compile to JavaScript numbers, but larger values will be truncated to 32 bits.

For example, the following code to output the truncated value 1445688163, not 1659303064419 as we would expect:

```
let add1 = (x: int) => x + 1
```

```
%%raw(`
// some large 64 bit number
let x = 1659303064418;
console.log(add1(x));
`)
```

On the other hand, floats will not be truncated, giving us the desired output:

```
let add1 = (x: float) => x +. 1.
```

```
%%raw(`
// some large 64 bit number
let x = 1659303064418;
console.log(add1(x));
`)
```

This means that large numbers like timestamps should generally be handled as floats to avoid any unexpected truncation.

Functions

Trying to partially apply an imported JavaScript function in ReScript may cause a runtime failure. This usually only happens in situations when we call functions without any defined bindings, but it is good to be aware of.

For example, the following code is an unsafe call to NodeJS's path. join function:

```
%%raw(`
var path = require('path');
`)
@val external path: 'a = "path"

let joined = path["join"]("a", "b")
Js.log(joined)
```

It compiles to the following JavaScript:

```
var Curry = require("rescript/lib/js/curry.js");

var joined = Curry._2(path.join, "a", "b");

console.log(joined);
```

Running the code will throw an exception at runtime:

```
.../node_modules/rescript/lib/js/curry.js:14
    return f.apply(null, args);
         ^

TypeError: f.apply is not a function
```

The solution to this is to force the call to be uncurried by putting a **.** in front of the arguments:

```
%%raw(`
var path = require('path');
`)
@val external path: 'a = "path"

let joined = path["join"](. "a", "b")
Js.log(joined)
```

This makes the generated code apply the arguments normally:

```
var joined = path.join("a", "b");

console.log(joined);
```

The code now successfully runs:

```
a/b
```

Problems with currying should be rare, but they are easy to spot and fix. When debugging a potential currying problem, search the generated JavaScript code for `Curry`, and fix the problem by making the call site or function definition uncurried.

Options

Options have no runtime wrapper, and compile to either the value (if present) or undefined if not. The lack of a runtime wrapper makes options easy to work with – if we want to use an optional value passed from ReScript, just check to see if it's undefined first and then we can use it directly:

```
let x = Some(1)
let y = None

Js.log(x)
Js.log(y)
```

Console output:

```
1
undefined
```

Other Data Types

Some of the data types that we discussed in the earlier chapters do not have a 1:1 equivalent in JavaScript, such as

Most collections (maps, sets, lists, etc.)

Variants

Immutable Data Structures

Maps, sets, and lists are JavaScript objects at runtime, but they may be deeply nested and difficult to read if we try to print them for debugging. They also should not be directly serialized into JSON. The best approach is to convert them to arrays using `toArray` before printing or serializing them, although be aware that frequent conversions of large collections can be expensive.

Variants

Variants which do not have data associated with them will compile to a number corresponding to the tag. Which number is associated with which tag depends on the order the tags are declared in. For example, in the variant type `type color = White | Black`, `White` compiles to 0 and `Black` compiles to 1.

The runtime representation of a variant with associated data is a JavaScript object, with the special TAG property containing the tag number and the associated data is stored in other special properties. Those properties _0, _1, _2, etc. may be present depending on how many pieces of data are associated with the tag. If the data associated with a tag is a single value or some other data type like an array or record, that value is stored in _0.

Let's demonstrate this using a simple variant type:

```
type entity = Player(string, int) | Enemy(int)
```

The expression Player("Danny", 10) compiles to:

```
{
  TAG: 0,
  _0: "Danny",
  _1: 10
}
```

The expression Enemy(10) compiles to:

```
{
  TAG: 1,
  _0: 10
}
```

Let's see how we would manipulate these values from JavaScript by writing a JavaScript function that takes an entity and returns a new entity with increased health:

```
%%raw(`
function addHealth(e, n) {
    if (e.TAG === 0) {
        return {TAG: 0, _0: e._0, _1: e._1 + n};
    } else if (e.TAG === 1) {
```

```
        return {TAG: 1, _0: e._0 + n};
    }
}
`)
@val
external addHealth: (entity, int) => entity = "addHealth"
```

Calling this function and inspecting the console reveals the structure of the variant data type:

```
let entity1 = Player("Danny", 10)
entity1->Js.log
entity1->addHealth(5)->Js.log

let entity2 = Enemy(5)
entity2->Js.log
entity2->addHealth(5)->Js.log
```

Console output:

```
{ TAG: 0, _0: 'Danny', _1: 10 }
{ TAG: 0, _0: 'Danny', _1: 15 }
{ TAG: 1, _0: 5 }
{ TAG: 1, _0: 10 }
```

As you can see, it is pretty difficult to work with variants directly in JavaScript, because we have to be aware of a lot of low-level details about how variants are represented.

In general, most logic dealing with variants should be kept within ReScript code, and variants that need to be passed to JavaScript should represent their data using more convenient data types such as records or arrays, which can be unwrapped before passing.

Polymorphic Variants

Polymorphic variants are an advanced feature of ReScript. Unlike regular variants which compile to numbers, polymorphic variants compile to the name of the tag. This makes them useful for representing static constants such as enums.

Polymorphic variant declarations look a bit different from regular variants – the tags are surrounded by square brackets and tag names are prefixed with #:

```
type color = [ #Black | #White ]
```

With the preceding polymorphic variant, the value #White compiles to the string literal "White" and #Black compiles to "Black." If the tag name is a number (e.g., #100), then the variant value will compile to a number literal as well.

Polymorphic variants with associated data still compile to objects like regular variants, but structure of the object is from regular variants. The tag name is stored as a string in the NAME property, while all the data associated with the tag is stored in the VAL property.

Here's the player/enemy example from before, rewritten using polymorphic variants:

```
type entity = [ #Player(string, int) | #Enemy(int) ]
%%raw(`
function addHealth(entity, n) {
    if (entity.NAME === "Player") {
        return {NAME: "Player", VAL: [entity.VAL[0], entity.
        VAL[1] + n]};
    } else if (entity.NAME === "Enemy") {
        return {NAME: "Enemy", VAL: entity.VAL + n};
    }
}
`)
```

```
@val
external addHealth: (entity, int) => entity = "addHealth"

let entity1 = #Player("Danny", 10)
entity1->Js.log
entity1->addHealth(5)->Js.log

let entity2 = #Enemy(5)
entity2->Js.log
entity2->addHealth(5)->Js.log
```

Running the code and inspecting the output reveals the underlying structure of our polymorphic variants:

```
{ NAME: 'Player', VAL: ['Danny', 10] }
{ NAME: 'Player', VAL: ['Danny', 15] }
{ NAME: 'Enemy', VAL: 5 }
{ NAME: 'Enemy', VAL: 10 }
```

Thanks to their superior readability when compiled, polymorphic variants are better than regular variants for writing interoperable code. The data is easier to unwrap when passing from ReScript to JavaScript, and the tag names are more readable when we need to write JavaScript code that works with variants.

Working with Null

One of the big advantages of ReScript over JavaScript is null safety via options. However, recall that the optional value None is actually undefined at runtime, not null.

Normally we don't need to deal with null values directly in ReScript, but the distinction between null and undefined matters when we pass possibly null or possibly undefined values from JavaScript to ReScript, or if we need to return a nullable value to JavaScript.

The standard library module Js.Nullable allows us to handle nulls in ReScript. Using this module, we can represent null in ReScript as Js.Nullable.null. Similarly, undefined and non-null values can be represented using this module:

```
let _ = Js.Nullable.null
let _ = Js.Nullable.undefined
let _ = Js.Nullable.return(1)
```

Note that the Js.Nullable type is a different type than the option type – the former represents a value that could be undefined or null, whereas the latter represents values that could be undefined but can never be null.

We can convert between nullable and option by using Js.Nullable. fromOption and Js.Nullable.toOption – when converting from nullable to option, null gets converted into None/undefined:

```
let null: Js.Nullable.t<int> = Js.Nullable.null

let option: option<int> = Js.Nullable.toOption(null)

Js.log(option)
Js.log(option === None)
```

Console output:

```
undefined
true
```

Use Js.Nullable.t as the parameter or return type where appropriate when binding to JavaScript functions that accept nullable inputs or return nullable values:

```
%%raw(`

function testNullable(input) {
    if (input === null) {
        console.log("the value is null");
    } else if (input == undefined) {
        console.log("the value is undefined");
    } else {
        console.log("the value is " + input);
    }
}

`)
```

```
@val
external testNullable: Js.Nullable.t<int> => unit =
"testNullable"
```

```
testNullable(Js.Nullable.null)
testNullable(Js.Nullable.undefined)
testNullable(Js.Nullable.return(1))
testNullable(Js.Nullable.fromOption(Some(1)))
testNullable(Js.Nullable.fromOption(None))
```

Console output:

```
the value is null
the value is undefined
the value is 1
the value is 1
the value is undefined
```

Working with Exceptions

ReScript's exceptions are a little different from exceptions thrown and caught in regular JavaScript code. Although overusing exceptions is bad, sometimes it is necessary for Rescript to interoperate with JavaScript exceptions. Utilities for working with JavaScript exceptions are found in the Js.Exn module.

Catching ReScript Exceptions in JavaScript

ReScript exceptions can be caught by JavaScript. For a particular caught exception e, the name of the exception can be found at e.RE_EXN_ID, and the stack trace can be found in e.Error.stack:

```
let foo = () => {
 raise(Not_found)
}

%%raw(`
try {
 foo();
} catch (e) {
 console.log(e.RE_EXN_ID);
}
`)
```

Console output:

```
Not_found
```

Extra information associated with a ReScript exception can be accessed in the exception object in a similar fashion as with variants.

For example, given the definition exception MyException(string), catching MyException("foo") in JavaScript yields the following object (the first positional argument is in _1, the second is in _2, etc.):

```
{
  RE_EXN_ID: "MyException",
  _1: "Foo",
  Error: ... // error object containing trace information
}
```

Given the definition exception CustomException({customMessage: string}), catching CustomException({customMessage: "foo"}) in JavaScript yields the following object, allowing us to easily access named fields in custom exceptions:

```
{
  RE_EXN_ID: "CustomException",
  customMessage: "Foo",
  Error: ... // error object containing trace information
}
```

We can also throw a generic JavaScript exception from Rescript using Js.Exn.raiseError:

```
let foo = () => {
 Js.Exn.raiseError("oh no")
}

%%raw(`
try {
 foo();
} catch (e) {
 console.log(e.message);
}
`)
```

Console output:

```
oh no
```

Catching JavaScript Exceptions in ReScript

When we want to use ReScript to call certain JavaScript APIs that may throw, we can handle possible exceptions using try/catch or pattern matching. JavaScript exceptions can be matched with `Js.Exn.Error`, and handling for JavaScript exceptions can be mixed with handling for regular ReScript exceptions.

Here's how we would catch a JavaScript exception from ReScript:

```
try {
  Js.Exn.raiseError("oh no")
} catch {
| Js.Exn.Error(e) => e->Js.Exn.message->Js.log
}
```

Working with JSON

There are several ways of serializing and deserializing JSON in ReScript, with different levels of convenience and type safety.

Option 1: Binding Without Types

The quick and dirty way to parse JSON is by writing a binding for `JSON.parse` with the `'a` return type. With that binding, we can parse arbitrary JSON strings and access the parsed object however we want. This is the least-safe option for JSON parsing in ReScript:

```
@scope("JSON") @val
external parse: string => 'a = "parse"
```

The inferred types for the parsed object are entirely based on what fields we access and how we use them, which grants us the flexibility to parse anything we want and access whatever values we want without worrying about writing types:

```
let parsed = parse(`{ "name": "Creamsicle", "age": 13, "owner":
"Danny" }`)
Js.log(parsed["name"])

let parsed = parse(`{ "player": 1, "score": 200}`)
Js.log(parsed["score"])
```

This is very nice for prototyping, but comes at the cost of type safety: the type system does not know what type the parsed object is, and does not do any validation to see if the JSON object is actually what we expect.

The compiler will not stop us from accessing a field that does not exist (whose value is undefined at runtime):

```
let parsed = parse(`{ "player": 1, "score": 200}`)
Js.log(parsed["hello"])
```

Console output:

```
undefined
```

Nor will it stop us from lying to the compiler about what type it is:

```
let parsed = parse(`{ "player": 1, "score": 200}`)
let x: string = parsed["hello"]
```

This can result in incorrect values polluting our otherwise safe code, causing errors to be thrown in unexpected places in our program. While this approach is very flexible, it's also quite unsafe – about as unsafe as parsing JSON in regular JavaScript.

Option 2: Binding With Types

One way to make JSON parsing safer is to write a type for the parsed object, and write separate bindings for each type of object that needs to be parsed. The type signature can be anything, but commonly it will be an object, record, or Dict:

```
type player = {
    "player": int,
    "score": int,
}

@scope("JSON") @val
external parsePlayer: string => player = "parse"

let parsed = parsePlayer(`{ "player": 1, "score": 200}`)
Js.log(parsed["score"])
```

Console output:

```
200
```

Now, if we use our custom parsePlayer binding to parse the JSON, the compiler will prevent us from accessing undefined properties from the parsed object:

```
Js.log(parsed["hello"])
```

Compiler output:

```
 This expression has type player
It has no method hello
```

While this is a nice upgrade, it only solves part of the problem. Since parsePlayer takes in arbitrary strings, there is nothing to stop us from passing in strings that do not correspond to the specified type.

The following example shows that this is still unsafe, because we can to trick the compiler into thinking that score is an int when in fact it is undefined:

```
type player = {
    "player": int,
    "score": int,
}

@scope("JSON") @val
external parsePlayer: string => player = "parse"

let parsed = parsePlayer(`{ "player": 1}`)
let score: int = parsed["score"]
```

While unexpected values at runtime might feel normal to someone coming from JavaScript, parsing JSON does not have to be this unsafe in ReScript. Let's see look at a safer way to parse JSON using ReScript's standard library.

Option 3: With Validation

Safe JSON parsing in ReScript is supported by the Js.Json standard library. Using it, we can write functions to parse JSON values and validate if the input string actually corresponds to the object that we expect. Errors can be caught and handled when the JSON string is parsed, instead of when we try to use the parsed value.

Although this requires writing a custom parsing function for each object type we want to parse, this approach gives us the highest level of control and safety.

```
let parsePlayer = (s: string) => {
 open Belt.Option
 let parsed = Js.Json.parseExn(s)
```

```
let obj = Js.Json.decodeObject(parsed)->getExn
let player = obj->Js.Dict.get("player")->flatMap(Js.Json.
decodeNumber)->getExn->Belt.Float.toInt
let score = obj->Js.Dict.get("score")->flatMap(Js.Json.
decodeNumber)->getExn->Belt.Float.toInt
{
  "player": player,
  "score": score,
}
}

let parsed = parsePlayer(`{ "player": 1}`)
```

Running the preceding program at runtime throws a Not_Found exception, because the "score" field does not exist in the JSON we are parsing:

```
RE_EXN_ID: 'Not_found',
Error: Error
```

To prevent runtime exceptions, we can just catch any exceptions inside the function and make it return an optional value, returning None if we fail to parse instead of crashing the program:

```
let parsePlayer = (s: string) => {
 open Belt.Option
 try {
   let parsed = Js.Json.parseExn(s)
   let obj = Js.Json.decodeObject(parsed)->getExn
   let player = obj->Js.Dict.get("player")->flatMap(Js.Json.
   decodeNumber)->map(Belt.Float.toInt)
   let score = obj->Js.Dict.get("score")->flatMap(Js.Json.
   decodeNumber)->map(Belt.Float.toInt)
```

```
  Some({
    "player": player->getExn,
    "score": score->getExn,
  })
} catch {
| _ => None
}
}

let parsed = parsePlayer(`{ "player": 1}`)

switch parsed {
| Some(_) => Js.log("we parsed it :)")
| _ => Js.log("failed to parse :(")
}
```

Console output:

```
failed to parse :(
```

We can further customize our parsing behavior by returning a result with a custom error message to aid debugging:

```
let parsePlayer = (s: string): result<player, string> => {
  open Belt
  let parsed = try {
    Ok(Js.Json.parseExn(s))
  } catch {
  | _ => Error("could not parse")
  }

  parsed
  ->Result.flatMap(p =>
    switch Js.Json.decodeObject(p) {
    | Some(o) => Ok(o)
```

```
    | None => Error("expected object")
    }
  )
  ->Result.flatMap(obj => {
    let player =
      obj->Js.Dict.get("player")->Option.flatMap(Js.Json.
      decodeNumber)->Option.map(Float.toInt)
    let score =
      obj->Js.Dict.get("player")->Option.flatMap(Js.Json.
      decodeNumber)->Option.map(Float.toInt)
    switch (player, score) {
    | (None, _) => Error("expected player:int")
    | (_, None) => Error("expected score:int")
    | (p, s) =>
      Ok({
        "player": p,
        "score": s,
      })
    }
  })
}

let parsed = parsePlayer(`{ "player": 1}`)
switch parsed {
| Ok(result) => Js.log(result)
| Error(message) => Js.log(message)
}
```

Console output:

```
expected score:int
```

Although this manual parsing code is quite cumbersome to write, it provides a lot of safety benefits by validating our payload before we try to use it. Luckily, when writing large-scale applications, there are various third-party libraries we can use to generate this code for us.

Putting It All Together: Simple ReScript Web App

To put together everything we've discussed in this chapter, let's create a web app from scratch. The app is very simple and consists of a client and server component, both written entirely in ReScript:

> The server will be a simple Express server providing an endpoint that takes in a name and returns a greeting for that name.

> The client will have an input to enter the name, a button to make a request to the server with the name, and some code to display the server's response on the web page.

We'll build two versions of the app, to show different ways to develop with ReScript:

1. First, we'll write handwritten bindings for the external functions that we use, to demonstrate how to write bindings to a variety of external APIs.

2. Next, we'll implement the same thing using prewritten bindings from a package, to demonstrate how we can use other people's bindings in our own code.

The second example is ideally how someone would write a web application in ReScript, but since not every JavaScript library has ReScript bindings, we sometimes have to fall back to the techniques in the first example to write our own bindings.

Version 1: Handwritten Bindings

Although ReScript bindings exist for Express, Node, and the DOM, we'll be writing everything from scratch in this example to demonstrate how to write bindings. Once we finish with both examples, compare the bindings we wrote to the ones we imported. Also keep in mind that there isn't a single correct way to write bindings – a particular function or value might be bound to different types in different use cases, depending on what is safest and most ergonomic.

Before we begin coding, we need to set up a new ReScript project. Refer to the first chapter for detailed instructions if necessary. We will also need to install the express package for our server:

```
npm install express
```

In our project directory, we will create four files:

> index.html
>
> Client.res
>
> Client.resi
>
> Server.res

Client

First, we'll make the HTML page that our application will display. Create an index.html file with the following contents:

```html
<!DOCTYPE html>
<html lang="en">

<head>
    <meta charset="UTF-8" />
    <meta name="viewport" content="width=device-width, initial-
    scale=1.0" />
</head>

<body>
    <h1>ReScript web app Demo</h1>
    <p>Enter Your Name:</p>
    <input id="name" type="text"/>
    <button id="submit">Submit</button>
    <p id="result"></p>
    <script type="text/javascript" src="./script"></script>
</body>

</html>
```

Next, we'll write the client-side code that will be loaded with the web page. This code will go inside Client.res. The corresponding interface Client.resi will be completely empty, which means the compiled JavaScript won't export any values.

The client code adds a listener to the submit button; when the button is clicked, it will read the contents of the text input and send a request to the server. Once the server responds, it will take the response and display it on the web page by modifying the innerHTML of our result element.

If we were to implement this using JavaScript, it would look something like this:

```javascript
var submit = document.getElementById("submit");
var result = document.getElementById("result");
var input = document.getElementById("name");
```

```
submit.addEventListener("click", param => {
    var payload = {
        method: "POST",
        headers: {
            Accept: "application/json",
            "Content-Type": "application/json"
        },
        body: JSON.stringify({
            name: input.value
        })
    };
    fetch("/hello", payload)
    .then(val => Promise.resolve(val.json()))
    .then(val => {
        result.innerHTML = val.message;
    });
});
```

To implement this from scratch in ReScript, we need to start by writing bindings for the client code.

For the DOM, there are several different types of bindings we'll make:

Globals: document

Functions/methods: getElementById, addEventListener, fetch

Object properties: value, innerHTML

The binding for document uses the standard library type Dom.document. Although ReScript's standard library provides type names for DOM elements, it doesn't provide any definitions – they're purely there for us to use when we write our own bindings:

```
@val external document: Dom.document = "document"
```

To access elements on the page, we use getElementById:

```
@send external getElementById: (Dom.document, string) => Dom.
element = "getElementById"
```

In JavaScript, this is a method that takes in a string and returns an element. Here, our binding takes in a Dom.document in addition to the string. This allows us to use the pipe operator to emulate JavaScript's method call syntax:

```
let element = document->getElementById("blah")
```

Notice the @send annotation on the binding. This lets the ReScript compiler know that we are binding to a method. With this annotation, function calls like x->f(y) or f(x, y) get compiled to x.f(y). Without the annotation, it would get compiled like a normal function, to f(x, y).

We'll also provide bindings for the element's addEventListener method the same way:

```
@send external addEventListener: (Dom.element, string, unit =>
unit) => unit = "addEventListener"
```

In our code, we also need to access the value property of the input element, and set the innerHTML property of another element. One way to do this is to model these properties as getter and setter functions, using the @get and @set annotations:

```
@get external getValue: Dom.element => string = "value"
@set external setInnerHTML: (Dom.element, string) => unit =
"innerHTML"
```

The @get annotation causes x->f and f(x) to be compiled to x.f, while the @set annotation causes x->f(y) and f(x, y) to be compiled to x.f = y. The two external functions can be called as such:

```
let value = element->getValue
element->setInnerHTML("blah")
```

Next, we'll write bindings for the fetch API. This is a global function that takes in a URL and a payload, and returns a promise for the response:

```
type response
@val external fetch: (string, 'a) => Js.Promise.t<response>
= "fetch"
```

The response object has a json method which allows us to extract the JSON payload. This method should return a JavaScript object, which we may not know the exact shape of.

In this situation, we can represent the object as a Dict whose values are Js.Json.t. When we access the dict and use its values, those values will need to be coerced into the expected types using functions such as Js.Json.decodeString.

```
@send external json: response => Js.Dict.t<Js.Json.t> = "json"
```

All together, the fetch API call and response handling looks like this:

```
 open Js.Promise
open Belt.Option
open Js.Json
fetch("/hello", payload)
->then_(response => response->json->resolve, _)
->then_(json => {
  let message = Js.Dict.get(json, "message")-
>flatMap(decodeString)->getExn
  result->setInnerHTML(message)
  resolve()
}, _)
->ignore
```

With all our bindings, the client-side code in ReScript looks like this:

```
@val external document: Dom.document = "document"
@send external getElementById: (Dom.document, string) => Dom.
element = "getElementById"

@send external addEventListener: (Dom.element, string, unit =>
unit) => unit = "addEventListener"

@get external getValue: Dom.element => string = "value"
@set external setInnerHTML: (Dom.element, string) => unit =
"innerHTML"

type response
@val external fetch: (string, 'a) => Js.Promise.t<response>
= "fetch"
@send external json: response => Js.Json.t = "json"

let submit = document->getElementById("submit")
let result = document->getElementById("result")
let input = document->getElementById("name")

submit->addEventListener("click", _ => {
  let payload = {
    "method": "POST",
    "headers": {
      "Accept": "application/json",
      "Content-Type": "application/json",
    },
    "body": Js.Json.stringifyAny({
      "name": input->getValue,
    }),
  }
  open Js.Promise
  open Belt.Option
```

```
open Js.Json
fetch("/hello", payload)
->then_(response => response->json->resolve, _)
->then_(json => json->decodeObject->getExn->resolve, _)
->then_(obj => {
  let message = Js.Dict.get(obj, "message")-
  >flatMap(decodeString)->getExn
  result->setInnerHTML(message)
  resolve()
}, _)
->ignore
})
```

Aside from the bindings, the ReScript implementation should look quite similar to the JavaScript implementation shown earlier.

Client Bundling

Since the client code has dependencies on ReScript's standard libraries, we need to use a bundler to include those dependencies in the code we send to the browser.

We'll use esbuild in this example since it is lightweight and fast, but in other projects feel free to use any bundler you want. To install esbuild, simply run the following:

```
npm install esbuild
```

We can add a command to run esbuild to our package.json; that way we don't have to remember any flags:

```
...
  "scripts": {
    "build": "rescript",
    "clean": "rescript clean -with-deps",
```

```
  "start": "rescript build -w",
  "esbuild": "esbuild src/Client.bs.js --outfile=src/Client.js
  --bundle"
},
...
```

Finally, we can compile and bundle the client code by running npm run build and npm run esbuild. The latter should take Client.bs.js and give us a bundled Client.js, which is what we'll load in the browser.

Server

For the server, we'll implement a simple Express web server in Server.res. It has three endpoints:

> / – Serves our web page
>
> /script – Serves the JavaScript file that is used by the web page
>
> /hello – Takes a JSON payload containing some text, prepends "Hello," to the text, and returns a JSON payload with the result

The server would look something like this if we implemented it in JavaScript:

```
var app = express();

app.use(express.json());

app.get("/", (param, response) =>
   response.sendFile(path.join(__dirname, "index.html"));
);
```

```
app.get("/script", (param, response) =>
  response.sendFile(path.join(__dirname, "Client.js"));
);

app.post("/hello", (request, response) =>
  response.send({
    message: "Hello, " + request.body.name
  });
);

app.listen(4000, param => console.log("Server running on port
4000."));

exports.app = app;
```

To implement this safely in ReScript, we'll need to have bindings for all the node and Express APIs that we use. As with the client code, this time we will write all the bindings from scratch.

First off, let's define a type for our app, and bind to the express module:

```
type app
@module external express: unit => app = "express"
```

Using the @module annotation allows us to bind to the entire module and use it as a function that returns a value of type app, as such:

```
let app: app = express()
```

We'll also need to bind to a function in the express module for the JSON middleware express.json(). To do that, we'll create a middleware type for this value. Binding to a function in a module also uses @module annotation, with some extra information specifying which module we're binding to:

```
type middleware
@module("express") external json: unit => middleware = "json"
```

To use the middleware, we need to call `app.use`. This is a regular method on the app object, so we'll bind to it using @send:

```
@send external use: (app, middleware) => unit = "use"
```

With that binding, the ReScript call `app->use(json())` compiles to `app.use(express.json())`.

Besides use, there are a couple more methods on the app object: get, post, and listen. We'll write bindings for those in the same way as we did for use. We'll also declare two new types to represent the request and response:

```
type request
type response

@send external get: (app, string, (request, response) => unit)
=> unit = "get"
@send external post: (app, string, (request, response) => unit)
=> unit = "post"
@send external listen: (app, int, unit => unit) => unit =
"listen"
```

The request has a body property that we need to access:

```
@get external getBody: request => 'a = "body"
```

It will be used like this:

```
app->post("/hello", (request, response) => {
 let body = request->getBody
  ...
})
```

The response has send and sendFile methods. For send, we use 'a to allow us to send back arbitrary JSON payloads:

```
@send external sendFile: (response, string) => unit = "sendFile"
@send external send: (response, 'a) => unit = "send"
```

As a more type-safe alternative, we could also write a binding that accepts a specific type for the payload, and share that type with the client.

Finally, we'll write bindings for node's file system operations: __ dirname and path.join().

We can model dirname as a regular external value:

```
@val external dirname: string = "__dirname"
```

Normally, path.join() is a variadic function that takes in an arbitrary number of strings. ReScript doesn't have variadic functions by default, but we can model variadic functions in our bindings by making the argument a single array of strings and using the @variadic annotation.

At runtime, the elements of the array will get unpacked and passed into the variadic function we are binding to – this is how Js.logMany([a, b, c]) unwraps to console.log(a, b, c).

We'll also use the @module annotation the same way we did for express.json():

```
@module("path") @variadic
external join: array<string> => string = "join"
```

We can call our new binding with join([x, y, z]), which will be compiled to path.join(x, y, z).

Here's an example of how we'll use the join binding together with dirname and sendFile:

```
app->get("/", (_, response) => {
 response->sendFile(join([dirname, "index.html"]))
})
```

The compiled output unwraps the variadic arguments as expected:

```
app.get("/", (function (param, response) {
    response.sendFile(Path.join(__dirname, "index.html"));
  }));
```

Aside, in this case since we only need path.join to join two strings, it would have also been acceptable to bind it as a regular function with two parameters.

The final result for our server code looks something like this:

```
type app
type middleware
type request
type response

@module external express: unit => app = "express"
@module("express") external json: unit => middleware = "json"

@send external use: (app, middleware) => unit = "use"
@send external get: (app, string, (request, response) => unit)
=> unit = "get"
@send external post: (app, string, (request, response) => unit)
=> unit = "post"
@send external listen: (app, int, unit => unit) => unit =
"listen"

@get external getBody: request => 'a = "body"

@send external sendFile: (response, string) => unit =
"sendFile"
@send external send: (response, 'a) => unit = "send"

@val external dirname: string = "__dirname"

@module("path") @variadic
```

```
external join: array<string> => string = "join"

let app = express()

app->use(json())

app->get("/", (_, response) => {
 response->sendFile(join([dirname, "index.html"]))
})

app->get("/script", (_, response) => {
 response->sendFile(join([dirname, "Client.js"]))
})

app->post("/hello", (request, response) => {
 let body = request->getBody
 response->send({
   "message": "Hello, " ++ body["name"],
 })
})

app->listen(4000, () => {
 Js.log("Server is running on port 4000.")
})
```

Again, aside from the bindings, the code should look very similar to JavaScript.

Running the Demo

To run the code locally, simply compile the project and run Server.bs.js using node to start the web server. Then, open up localhost:4000 on your web browser, and you should see the web page.

Try typing your name and hitting the submit button, and see the results show up on screen. Congratulations, you've now built your first full-stack web application using ReScript!

In the next version, we'll replace our handwritten bindings with some prewritten bindings. Generally, if good prewritten bindings exist for a particular library, you should use them since it saves a lot of time. Handwriting bindings for everything is quite time-consuming, but it's sometimes necessary if there are no existing bindings, or if the existing bindings are not ergonomic for your specific use case.

Version 2: Using Imported Bindings

Now, let's reimplement our web app using some third-party bindings from rescript-webapi, rescript-nodejs, and rescript-express. First, install the bindings from npm:

```
npm install rescript-express
npm install rescript-webapi
npm install rescript-nodejs
```

We'll also need to add these dependencies under bs-dependencies in our project's bsconfig.json:

```
...
  "bs-dependencies": [
    "rescript-express",
    "rescript-webapi",
    "rescript-nodejs"
  ],
...
```

Client

Let's modify the client-side code to use external bindings.

First, we'll use destructuring to extract the functions we want from the binding modules. For the Webapi.Dom.HtmlInputElement module, we will also assign aliases to the generically named ofElement and value functions, so that our code is easier to read. If we were working with other element types, this aliasing would have been necessary to avoid shadowing:

```
let {document} = module(Webapi.Dom)
let {getExn, flatMap} = module(Belt.Option)
let {getElementById} = module(Webapi.Dom.Document)
```

```
let {addEventListener, setInnerHTML} = module(Webapi.Dom.
Element)
let {ofElement: getInput, value: inputValue} = module(Webapi.
Dom.HtmlInputElement)
```

The code that selects our DOM elements should look familiar. Each selection is piped into Belt.Option.getExn because getElementById returns an optional value (None if the element doesn't exist). Since we know the element exists, we will forcibly unwrap it.

The getElementById function returns a generic value compatible with Webapi.Dom.Element. That module only supports operations shared across all DOM elements, so in order to support input-specific operations such as reading the input value, we need to construct a value compatible with Webapi.Dom.HtmlInputElement using Webapi.Dom.HtmlInputElement. fromElement:

```
let submit = document->getElementById("submit")->getExn
let result = document->getElementById("result")->getExn
let input = document->getElementById("name")-
>flatMap(getInput)->getExn
```

Building the payload of the request using WebApi.Fetch is different from how we did it by hand; the API is much more structured and provides named parameters to ensure the request is well-formed:

```
submit->addEventListener("click", _ => {
 open Webapi.Fetch
 let payload = RequestInit.make(
   ~method_=Post,
   ~headers=HeadersInit.make({
     "Accept": "application/json",
     "Content-Type": "application/json",
   }),
```

```
  ~body=BodyInit.make(
    Js.Json.stringifyAny({
      "name": input->inputValue,
    })->getExn,
  ),
  (),
 )
 ...
}
```

Finally, we use `Webapi.Fetch.fetchWithInit` API to make the request. Like our handwritten binding, this API also returns a promise, and the result handling is similar to before:

```
open Js.Promise
fetchWithInit("/hello", payload)
->then_(Response.json, _)
->then_(json => json->Js.Json.decodeObject->getExn->resolve, _)
->then_(obj => {
  let message = Js.Dict.get(obj, "message")->flatMap(Js.Json.
decodeString)->getExn
  result->setInnerHTML(message)
  resolve()
}, _)
->ignore
```

The completed final version of our client-side code should look like this:

```
let {document} = module(Webapi.Dom)
let {getExn, flatMap} = module(Belt.Option)
let {getElementById} = module(Webapi.Dom.Document)
```

```
let {addEventListener, setInnerHTML} = module(Webapi.Dom.
Element)
let {ofElement: getInput, value: inputValue} = module(Webapi.
Dom.HtmlInputElement)

let submit = document->getElementById("submit")->getExn
let result = document->getElementById("result")->getExn
let input = document->getElementById("name")-
>flatMap(getInput)->getExn

submit->addEventListener("click", _ => {
 open Webapi.Fetch
 let payload = RequestInit.make(
   ~method_=Post,
   ~headers=HeadersInit.make({
     "Accept": "application/json",
     "Content-Type": "application/json",
   }),
   ~body=BodyInit.make(
     Js.Json.stringifyAny({
       "name": input->inputValue,
     })->getExn,
   ),
   (),
 )
 open Js.Promise
 fetchWithInit("/hello", payload)
 ->then_(Response.json, _)
 ->then_(json => json->Js.Json.decodeObject->getExn-
>resolve, _)
 ->then_(obj => {
```

```
    let message = Js.Dict.get(obj, "message")->flatMap(Js.Json.
    decodeString)->getExn
    result->setInnerHTML(message)
    resolve()
  }, _)
  ->ignore
})
```

Like the previous iteration, we'll also need to bundle it using esbuild.

Server

On the server side, the Express module from rescript-express provides most of the server bindings, while NodeJs module from rescript-nodejs provides the file system API.

At the top of our file, we'll destructure the Express module and extract the functions we need:

```
let {
  expressCjs: express,
  jsonMiddleware: json,
  listenWithCallback: listen,
  use,
  get,
  post,
  body,
  sendFile,
  send,
} = module(Express)
```

Since the whole file deals with Express server logic, it would have also been acceptable to just open Express at the top of the file.

Like we did for our client code, we can use aliases to give our imported functions better names: express instead of expressCjs and json instead of jsonMiddleware. By explicitly specifying the names, it's easier to avoid accidental shadowing, and we can rename awkwardly named API functions to better match the API name in JS.

Converting the endpoints to use the new APIs should be pretty straightforward:

```
app->get("/script", (_, response) => {
 open NodeJs
 response->sendFile(Path.join([Global.dirname, "Client.
js"]))->ignore
})
```

After all the API call sites have been updated, the server code for our final version should look like this:

```
let {
 expressCjs: express,
 jsonMiddleware: json,
 listenWithCallback: listen,
 use,
 get,
 post,
 body,
 sendFile,
 send,
} = module(Express)

let app = express()

app->use(json())
```

```
app->get("/", (_, response) => {
 open NodeJs
 response->sendFile(Path.join([Global.dirname, "index.
 html"]))->ignore
})

app->get("/script", (_, response) => {
 open NodeJs
 response->sendFile(Path.join([Global.dirname, "Client.
js"]))->ignore
})

app->post("/hello", (request, response) => {
 let body = request->body
 response
 ->send({
   "message": "Hello, " ++ body["name"],
 })
 ->ignore
})

let _ = app->listen(4000, _ => {
 Js.log("Server is running on port 4000.")
})
```

And now we're done! The new code leverages third-party bindings to allow us to safely use JavaScript libraries, without spending all day writing our own bindings.

Final Thoughts

You've learned how to prototype a full-stack web application in ReScript; write your own bindings for functions, objects, and modules; and also use bindings that other people have written.

The way that ReScript works gives a lot of flexibility in how we can use it. Writing a web application from scratch entirely in ReScript (like we just did) is just one way of using this language.

It's possible to integrate ReScript into an existing JavaScript or TypeScript application by writing a self-contained module in ReScript, or by incrementally rewriting parts of the old code base in ReScript. There are official guides to gradually adopt ReScript and integrate it into existing applications, and if you follow them, the migration process should be smooth and relatively nondisruptive.

While I don't provide any examples of migrating large code bases in this book, I recommend that you try it out if you have an old JavaScript or TypeScript project lying around. You'll get valuable practice using all of ReScript's nice features and get a better sense for how ReScript can help make web applications less buggy and safer to develop. Once the process is over, you'll have more peace of mind, thanks to the additional safety guarantees that ReScript provides.

It's also worth mentioning that although the front end of our demo was just a simple HTML page, it's possible to use ReScript with a number of common front-end web frameworks – in particular, readers intending to use ReScript for front-end web development will be delighted to learn that ReScript has excellent first-class support and integration with React, including the ability to write JSX directly in ReScript files. React is out of scope for this book, but you can find details on ReScript's first-class bindings for React and JSX in the official documentation.

Lastly, the functional programming concepts in this book don't just apply to programming in ReScript. Even when working in a language without features like type inference and pattern matching, we can still think about programming in terms of immutability, composability, and side effects to make our code cleaner, safer, and more maintainable.

Index

A

Arguments, 8, 24, 25, 31, 36–43, 65, 119, 194, 215, 244
Arithmetic operators, 3, 4
Array.map API, 34
Arrays
    access, 111–113
    angle brackets, 110
    generic type variables, 110
    higher-order functions (*see* Higher-order functions, arrays)
    JavaScript, 109, 110
    Js.Array2, 110
    luggage array, 124
    operations, JavaScript, 111
    push method, 111, 137
    standard library functions, 110

B

Belt.Array library, 127
Belt.Array.getExn function, 42, 43
Belt.HashSet, 141, 171
Belt.Int.toString, 32, 33, 84
Belt.List standard library, 132, 133

Belt.Map, 141, 143, 146, 150, 161, 170, 172, 185
Belt.MutableMap, 141, 161, 172
Belt.MutableSet, 141, 161
Belt.MutableStack, 141, 157
Belt.Option standard library module, 74
Belt.Option.flatMap functions, 74
Belt.Option.map functions, 74
Belt.Result module, 81
Belt.Set, 141, 143, 161, 171
Belt standard library, 112, 179
Bindings
    creation, 9
    external, 24, 247
    immutable, 10
    mutation, 12
    refs, 11, 12
    shadowing, 10
    tuples, 55
    types, 9
    values associations, 9
    variable let declarations, 9
Blocks, 12–14, 78, 84, 86, 207
Block scoping, 14, 15
Boolean, 5–7, 50, 52, 65, 70, 71, 97, 116

S

Printed in the United States
by Baker & Taylor Publisher Services